All Heart

The Baseball Life of
Frank Torre

Other books by Cornelius Geary:

La Gitana & the Lady Bullfighters of Mexico
(y Señoritas Toreras Mexicanas)
(with Sandra Martinez Geary)

All Heart

The Baseball Life
of Frank Torre

as told to
Cornelius Geary

HenschelHAUS Publishing, Inc.
Milwaukee, Wisconsin

Unless otherwise credited, photographs are provided courtesy of Richard Lulloff from his collection.

Published by
HenschelHAUS Publishing, Inc.
2625 S. Greeley St. Suite 201
Milwaukee, WI 53207
www.henschelhausbooks.com
Please contact HenschelHAUS for information about quantity discounts.

ISBN (paperback): 978159598-697-9
ISBN (hardcover): 978159598731-0
E-ISBN: 978159598-698-6
Audio ISBN: 978159598-711-2
LCCN: 2019930377

Printed in the United States of America

*This book is dedicated to the memory of Neil and Sara Geary,
and to Mike, Mary Eileen, Tim, Dan, Terry, Madeline,
and Tom, with whom I shared the 1950s and '60s,
a glass of water, and a toothbrush.*

Contents

Warm-up (Acknowledgments) 1

First Pitch (Introduction) 3

Dear Old Dad 9

The Glory Years 35

1958: The Kiss of Death....................................... 117

Rarities 159

1959: One High Hop.. 167

1960: Sideways... 175

Ace of Hearts.. 185

Extra Inning.. 203

The Legend of Mel Fame 205

Appendix.. 207

Index 209

About the Author 215

Warm-Up
(Acknowledgments)

I T WAS PERHAPS JUST PURE COINCIDENCE that Frank Torre and I connected, which resulted in his willingness to convey his baseball life into a tape recorder and onto these pages. First and foremost, I am grateful to the great Milwaukee Braves first baseman, Frank Torre, a true world champion, for his time, thoughtfulness, and candor in telling his story.

This book would not have nearly the depth or visual appeal that it does without the use of Milwaukee Braves and other historical baseball photographs kindly made available by Richard Lulloff, a fine collector of Wisconsin sports material. I'm also grateful to his brother Tom for connecting me with Richard. Many thanks to them both.

I'm also very appreciative of Rick Schabowski, a Milwaukee sports historian and author, for his very helpful review and comments on the manuscript.

Thanks also to Milwaukee native Robert Reuteman, writer, editor, and adjunct professor of business journalism at Colorado State University, for his initial review of the manuscript, sage insights, and high editorial standard. Thanks, Rob.

I'm also obviously most appreciative of our fine publisher, Kira Henschel, the proprietor of HenschelHAUS, for her enlightened view toward publishing Frank's story and her support throughout the publishing process. It is only fitting that after several earlier attempts to find the right publisher, we were best able to do it with a publisher based in Milwaukee.

I'd also like to thank my son Con Geary, also a Cornelius, for his love of baseball and continual focus on the game and its never-ending evolution. I believe he has my collection of original Milwaukee Braves baseball cards in safe custody. I appreciate his comments on the manuscript.

I'm also exceptionally grateful for the advice of old friend John Smith, a true Milwaukeean and a great Wisconsin sports fan, who urged me to stay in the hunt for the right publisher. That extra push did the trick.

Thanks to brother Dan Geary, who told me that a friend of his read the manuscript and said, "It's the best book I ever read." I want to buy that guy a drink, or at least lunch at George Webb's.

Finally, thanks to Sandra Martinez Geary, my wife, for her continued support and understanding as I disappear on the second floor for hours if not days at a time. All work and no play makes Jack a dull boy.

Without any of the above, including Con Geary, Liz Geary, and John Geary, for their infinite patience, and whose affections I cherish, this book would not be appearing.

Thanks to all!
Cornelius Geary

First Pitch
(Introduction)

THIS VERBATIM ACCOUNT OF MUCH of Frank Torre's life took shape early in the 21st century, initially in New York. Someone handed me Frank Torre's business card after meeting him. As a kid who grew up in Milwaukee in the 1950s, I was intrigued. It's not so much that Frank was an idol, but that all of the Braves were idols to us, including Frank, especially being seven years old the year the Braves won the World Series in 1957. I called the number on the card, not exactly knowing why, and Frank Torre came to the phone.

I told him where I was from and wondered if he'd mind getting together because I'd love to talk to him about the Milwaukee Braves. He said sure and we met in Ft. Lee, New Jersey, where he shared a business operation selling tickets to sports and theatrical events with his brother Joe. I asked him if he minded if I taped our conversation and he said, no. At one point, we drove out to the modest row house in Brooklyn where Frank and Joe were raised by their parents, where his sister Rae still lived, and where much of the early story imparted here took place.

Well, one thing led to another and shortly thereafter Frank agreed that I would visit him at his house in Palm Beach Gardens, Florida. He lived by himself in a nice gated community, near his kids and grandkids. I spent the greater part of a week with Frank, staying overnight, sleeping on the top bunk of a kid's bunkbed, and sharing corn flakes with him in the morning. We'd talk all day, me taping, and on into the night. For lunch, we'd ride a golf cart to the club house, and talk and tape some more in the afternoon. For dinner, Frank would rustle up some grub, usually a salad and chicken or pork chops.

Late afternoons and evenings were very interesting, as Frank often would have one of the *Godfather* movies playing in the background. He loved all three of the movies, and from time to time, we'd take a break, or Frank would ask me to pause the tape, because he was following a scene.

"Stop the tape," he'd say. "Fredo is about to get the kiss." Or, "That's just like it was in Brooklyn."

Frank was very cognizant of the Italian experience in America, and he felt the *Godfather* movies were a reasonably fair depiction of the people and culture he knew growing up. He felt the same way about the Sopranos.

Frank was justifiably proud of his life as a Milwaukee Brave. He had been very confident of his talent as a young baseball player, and in fact was considered to be one of the best players ever to come out of Brooklyn by many. Yet, at the same time he realized he was part of history, playing championship-caliber ball as teammate with the likes of Henry Aaron, Ed Mathews and Warren Spahn, and going up against greats like Willie Mays, Gil Hodges, Mickey Mantle, and Whitey Ford. He knew who the greats were, and he considered himself most worthy to be competing on the same fields. In terms of valuing his talent, he didn't take a back seat to anyone. As he explains here, he also felt he needed to be an everyday player in order to shine, especially on offense. His story bears that out.

With respect to the legendary baseball career of his younger brother, the great Joe Torre, Frank was more than proud. He also wanted to tell for the record his part in initiating Joe's career, which he does in this story. Frank recognized the tremendous irony of his winning a World Series Championship and the coveted ring that accompanies it in 1957, 39 years before Joe won his first championship and a World Series ring, with the New York Yankees in 1996.

After his major league career faded, Frank went on to have a successful life as a business executive, first with Andiron-dack, and then with Rawlings, maker of sports products and notably baseballs and baseball gloves. He achieved a number of major successes, including winning back the baseball franchise for Rawlings with Major League Baseball, and helping open up the Japanese market for all things baseball. Even as a businessman, Frank was a scrapper. He talked about working spring training with a traveling van that held a lathe, and shaping bats for players like Orlando Cepeda and Willie McCovey on the spot. He hung out and practiced fly fishing with Ted Williams at trade shows, where the Splendid Splinter spent an afterlife as a sports equipment marketer and spokesperson for Sears.

At the beginning, between his origins in Brooklyn and success in Milwaukee, Frank progressed up the usual minor league ladder, in Atlanta, Wichita, Toledo, and Denver. He recalls being assigned a hitting coach in the minor leagues, the Hall of Famer Paul Waner. In order to receive his batting instruction early in the day from this lifetime .333 hitter, Frank had to go to the boarding house and get Paul up out of bed. To get Paul up, he had to enter his room, and pour whiskey into the water glass. Before he poured whiskey into the glass, he needed to remove Mr. Waner's dentures. The first drink got Paul sitting up. In order to get Paul dressed and out the door, another glass of whiskey was required. Then they'd trundle over to the park, dragging a bag of balls and lugging bats for some lessons and practice swings.

Frank also served his country in the U.S. Army during the Korean War, wielding his steady glove and playing on rocky fields and pitching ship decks to entertain his fellow soldiers.

Frank talks in this tome about his own sometimes gruff temperament, which he acknowledged might be perceived as a bit too much on the tough side to some. He came from the streets and neighborhoods of Brooklyn, he'd seen both sides of the American dream, served in the Army, and knew what it took to get ahead in life. He didn't pull punches. But he was an astute observer of people, baseball and life. He was very kind at heart, well-intended in his comments, and always action and results-oriented. He also was very, very smart, and had a very sardonic sense of humor.

Regarding the content of this book, every word of it is directly from the mouth of Frank Torre. It has only been punctuated as necessary for ease of reading. As a story-teller, Frank spoke in a delightful Brooklyn stream-of-consciousness. His sentences would take flight, and in the original transcript there might not be a period for two pages. He might start out describing Brooklyn, send us to Iowa, take us through Korea, and land us back in Milwaukee. It is too bad he didn't get more radio and TV time in his own right, because he was a wonderful conversationalist. Early readers of an initial draft felt it would be more helpful to punctuate Frank's conversation more traditionally, so I've done so. As you read it, you'll also see that Frank had his own unique way with words.

If there are any errors of fact, however, they are entirely mine. In telling his story, Frank was drawing on recollections, many that were forty, fifty, even sixty years old, and I've endeavored, with the great help of Rick Schabowski, to fact-check dates, scores, outcomes. And frankly, forgiving that one pun, there were few corrections to be made, because Frank was right on in his memory almost 100 percent of the time.

The Milwaukee Braves were an important part of baseball history, and Frank Torre was a key player on the great Braves teams of the 1950s. There still exists today, partially as a result of the resurgence of the Milwaukee Brewers, great interest in looking back at the Braves. I think that Frank's perspective on those years makes an important contribution to the Milwaukee Braves, and therefore also, to baseball history.

One last note: Frank was very aware of all the ink and media coverage that his MVP and Hall of Fame brother Joe earned over the years. And he was more than proud of Joe. At the same time, Frank very much wanted to tell his own story, his way.

In that spirit, here it is, in his own words, *All Heart—The Baseball Life of Frank Torre*, as told to me, for which I am very grateful.

—Cornelius Geary

Dear Old Dad

OUR FATHER, KING JOE THE FIRST, was a tyrant, and abusive both physically and psychologically. He was a ticking time bomb. We never knew when he would explode.

What caused this trait to fester in him, we did not know. As the situation worsened, we didn't care much either. We simply had to deal with it.

Looking back, all we can attribute it to was his having been spoiled rotten by his family as he was growing up. He was an Italian prince. They brought him pillows for his head and back and footstools if he was not comfortable, and catered to his every whim.

He was fed like royalty. As a married adult, he expected this same kind of service from my mother.

My father became a member of the New York City police department. He was always in plain clothes and always kept very late hours. Whatever the hell he was doing by night, he would usually sleep until two or three in the afternoon.

During the day, we children weren't allowed to run the hot water until after he took his shower. I think that's why, even now I like baths so much, because if you got water at all then, it was only about a five-minute job. While my father slept, we had to stay very quiet, or there was hell to pay.

One very notable incident that captures the entire ordeal occurred when I was nineteen years old in our house on Avenue T in Brooklyn. This house had a basement with entrances front and back and we were conditioned to enter through these doors. That way, we wouldn't disturb the tense peace and quiet that existed on the floors above.

This one particular afternoon I came in through the basement as usual and I guess the folks upstairs didn't hear me as I came in. Immediately I could tell there was an argument going on up above, and then I heard a huge crash.

When my father got up in the afternoon, it was understood that my mother had to cook him his eggs a certain way—sunny side up. Apparently, this time she hadn't cooked the eggs exactly the way he wanted them. In his anger, he had taken the plate and thrown it up against the wall.

I came running upstairs. When I entered the kitchen, there was my father, the New York City cop, wielding a huge knife, waving it in his hand and threatening my mother with it. He was yelling at her. "If you ever screw up my eggs again, I'll use this knife on you." Mom was cowering in the corner, shaking and crying.

At the age of 19, I was 6 foot 3, 210 pounds, a minor league prospect, and certainly not afraid of the bully cop in the kitchen who was threatening my mother and who also happened to be my dad. I already had a bent nose that had been busted a few times on the playing field and on the street. I entered the fray without hesitation and shouted, "I'll take that knife and stick it up your ass. You ever touch my mother again, I'll kill you."

He knew I would take him on with or without the knife. Right away he clammed up and put the knife down.

There was a silence then and we all went back about our business. I scooped up the plate and the splattered eggs. Mom disappeared into the living room. Dad sat down with his coffee and toast, I guess prepared the way he liked them.

Dear Old Dad

My brother Joe recalls a different episode with a knife, and maybe that one took place too, but the incident with the eggs is what my sister, mother and I recall.

Even though Mom was scared to death, she just wasn't as frightened when I was around. She knew that if push came to shove, I would probably follow through. Even though dad was a tough guy, I was much bigger, and at that stage in my life, just as crazy as he was.

I had watched him abuse my mother for years. Not being able to do anything about it when we were real young was tough, but as I got bigger, I was anxious to act.

My Italian heritage in those days just presumed that the wife should stay home and take care of the children and the husband had the blessing to do almost anything and everything he wanted.

We Torre children on several occasions actually saw our father in our own neighborhood out and about with other women. My older brother Rocco and my sisters Marguerite and Rae got smacked around on account of it, as if seeing him had been their fault.

In essence, our father was living a double life. What that does to you as a person is hard to say. But deep inside, when you're basically living a lie like that, it disturbs you, and you do irrational and harmful things, even to those you presumably love.

As a police officer in those days, Dad made about $260 a month in regular pay. While this was decent middle class pay of the day, it was not a lot either, but he gave my mother the entire paycheck. Out of it she had to pay the mortgage, feed us, clothe us, everything. Money at home was tight.

So tight in fact, that later when I started to earn some money playing semi-pro ball, my brother Rocco would swipe it from me for his dates. No matter where I conspired to hide it, he found it. That's when I started sleeping with my socks on, so he couldn't get at my money.

The first time I was paid $50 for pitching, I was just a teen-ager, playing outfield on a semi-pro outfit sometimes backing up the likes of real pros such as Satchel Paige. I came home with the money and offered it to my mother and she turned it down. She didn't believe I could make that kind of money playing baseball. She thought I had stolen it.

Actually, Rocco was making off with my money. So I started turning the money over to Mom in smaller increments—$10 at a time—and sleeping in my socks to hide the dough from my brother.

There was a lot of corruption in the police department in those days, and unfortunately my father all but had no choice

The immortal Satchel Paige throwing for the Miami Marlins. A teenaged Frank Torre played the field for Paige-led teams at the Polo Grounds. Paige began his pitching career at Birmingham in 1927, and recorded his final out throwing in the Carolina League in 1966. He pitched in six American League seasons with Cleveland, St. Louis and Kansas City including in the 1948 World Series. He recorded a strike-out for KC in 1965 tossing three innings, giving up one hit.

except to be part of it. It was essentially an inescapable way of life for virtually everyone on the force. There was too much money involved.

I know for a fact of a police captain, way back then, who made $5,000 a month extra just for being a captain. This was when $5,000 was backed by silver and not thin air.

Another police captain was called Honest So-and-So, because he apparently wouldn't play along. Yet he too raked in five grand a month, and this was an honest officer. He didn't have to do anything except look the other way. That was a lot of money for not seeing anything.

Of course, the police department was involved in most anything that went on in the city, and those practices were pervasive. As such, my dad's affairs ranged pretty much all over the town.

Initially when he joined the force, we were told that he too had tried to avoid the dishonesty. As a result, he was shunned and soon had to come around in order to survive. With other income coming in and giving my mother his entire paycheck, he was off on his own.

That was the family arrangement, but inside, it pretty much ate away at him.

So we managed to get by. But every month was an adventure. While he went off to Florida for a month at a time, or was up in Saratoga, or running around God knows where, and keeping those crazy hours, Mom took in what we called "home work," which was sewing and crocheting. We all made the little money we had in the house stretch as far as possible.

Dad seemed to think he was giving us an unbelievable treat when occasionally in the summer he would take the whole family up to Saratoga. These were our get-away vacations. He would drop us off at a place called McNell's, a well-known resort in the Adirondacks, and he'd go off to the track or some of the tonier joints hidden away in the trees and hills. We wouldn't see him until it was time to go home.

His extra money gave him the latitude to sort of rise above his family. He basically orbited around us. He was an independent, even though he was married and we were his kids. He led a life with a lot of freedoms, but when he did show up at the house, he expected everything to be perfect.

I mean hell, that's how I learned to play cards real well and even learned to cook. He'd bring home these late night card games, showing up with a table full of guys in fedoras and shoulder holsters with cigars and pinky rings. Rather than having my mother stay up all night, serving and catering to his card games, I would step in and take care of it. "Do you want another sandwich? Do you want this? Do you want that?" I'd clean up afterwards and they'd toss me a few bucks for helping them out. I did this just so my mother could go to bed.

Sometimes these were school nights. The card games would go on in the house into the wee hours of the morning. These sharpies usually played gin rummy. I was street smart already, and I became acutely attuned to the action going on around me.

There would be my dad, with other members of the police force, and some other guys who were not, but always as I recall, high-level people, and these were serious games. Weapons hung over the chairs, and the occasional small firearm could be seen stuck inside a sock or up a pants-leg. While there were never any serious problems, I recall minor disputes over a hand or a winning streak, and a couple of guys exchanging glances.

There would be dead silence. Blue smoke. Somebody might glance at a weapon. I would freeze holding a plate of ham sandwiches. You could almost hear the breathing in the bedrooms upstairs. Then one guy laughed, and another guy laughed, and then everyone laughed, and the game went on. Real Joe Pesci stuff.

Only once did I ever actually see my father wearing a police uniform. This was at a ceremony near the end of his career. During all those years, I met police inspectors, judges, police captains. These were the people that I used to call "Uncle," the people dad rubbed elbows with most of the time, who shuffled the decks of cards in our house at all hours, and ate our food while the family tried to sleep above the coughing and the laughing.

This type of background and early childhood were largely responsible for my brother Joe being who he is today. Had he not been exposed to the types of things we were made to see, and the grief my mother endured, and the things she was deprived of, Joe wouldn't be Joe. It's that simple.

Joe was born at great sacrifice. My mother had lost a little girl a few years earlier. Against the demands of my father and the advice of the family doctor, she was bent on having another child. Therefore, when Joe was born, the old man was not pleased.

Joe became like an orphan to my father. He was ignored completely, or yelled at. As the poor kid grew up and realized what was happening to him for no reason whatsoever, it only got worse. The hazing or the silence only intensified.

Joe really was treated awfully by my father, verbally berated, criticized, and essentially abused. He couldn't do anything right. It got so if Joe saw the old man's car in the garage or on the street, he wouldn't come home. He'd wander away down the street.

Watching this happen to my little brother deeply penetrated my brain. Even though as children there was nothing we could do about the situation, I was determined if at all possible, to give Joe a chance to fulfill at least some of his dreams.

The one great escape from that tension and fear for all of us, including the girls, was sports, and especially baseball. The streets outside represented freedom where you could be judged on the basis of your effort or your skill. We spent as much time playing in the huge parks of Brooklyn nearby or on the streets as the daylight or the streetlights allowed.

Sunday dinner didn't start for us until our baseball games ended. Mom respected that. She might have a chicken dinner ready to go but if Rocco or I were playing extra innings, dinner was kept warm until we hustled in. Dad did not interfere. Playing outside for hour after hour helped us forget the scenes inside.

At a very early age, Joe pretty much showed us where he wanted to go with his life, and that was into baseball. He was a pretty well-rounded kid, decent in school, but baseball was his love.

At the same time, there were so many strikes working against him. Not only did the old man cast a heavy shadow over him, but he was terribly coddled by my mother and sisters. As a result, he had no apparent outward ambition, no noticeable drive or motivation.

Even worse, Joe was born with a great lack of speed on the base paths. On the surface, he didn't seem possessed of any outstanding athletic ability.

I gave the kid a lot of thought and spun my wheels quite a bit figuring out how best I might be able to give my brother a chance.

It was proven out later that even as he matured none of the pro scouts were interested or saw any realistic future prospect for him in baseball.

Dear Old Dad

We were ten years apart and I had never really seen Joe play ball much when he was young. When he was first coming into his own, I was always on the road in the minor leagues, or away in the service.

But when he was 15 years old, and the Braves came to town to play the Dodgers, he got the chance to work out with us at Ebbets Field. I saw right away that he had a good arm and that he could hit. He had a good stroke and some power with the bat. In certain categories, either as a pitcher or a catcher, that meant he might have a chance to play professional ball.

That's why I put a gun to his amateur coach's head, so to speak, to make sure Joe was made to play catcher after he graduated from high school, where he'd pitched a bit and played first and third.

Now as a teen, I had played with the Brooklyn Cadets, a local amateur baseball organization in Brooklyn. As kids, we spent many hours of our lives at Marine Park with the Cadets.

The Brooklyn Cadets still exist, because of people like Dan Hill, Jim McElroy, and probably myself and my brother Joe. There's a great tradition there and I'm proud to be part of it.

In 1949, my play was one of the reasons we went to Johnstown, Pennsylvania and won the national amateur tournament. I pitched two victories in two days and it was the first time that Brooklyn had ever won. This early success helped lift me out of the neighborhood and into the attention of the people in organized baseball. And later, that's what put me in position to help Joe.

Sensing that these same possibilities existed for Joe was probably the main reason that I used to be rather tough on him, that I was all over him, so to speak. Not physically, but I used to harass the hell out of him about his eating and how lazy and spoiled he was. He was going to have to break out of the

Frank Torre, right, returns as a major league star to join in a Brooklyn Cadets trophy presentation.

clutches of being battered (psychologically) by the old man on one hand and pampered to death by the ladies of the house on the other. He needed to cut himself a new path.

At the time I was banging on him, I didn't realize that the criticism was way over his head, and I was more than a little rough on him. I am known to be candid and blunt. Frankly, he really didn't understand, and it was basically my approach that turned him off.

I found out later that he disliked me, and maybe even hated me during a period of our lives, in part because of how tough I was on him. But all of these things were part of my intent to help him have an opportunity to play professional baseball.

The requirements for being a catcher then were a lot different, and they still are, than for almost any other position, different from almost anything else in professional sports.

Think, literally, of a backstop with an arm that can stand pain. You aren't required to run fast. You have to catch, have a good arm, and be able to take the pain. It helps to be able to hit. You can learn to know the hitters.

When Joe did sign a contract after switching to catcher and began to generate some interest, the Braves scout who signed him, Honey Russell,[1] who had also signed me, was widely ridiculed within the organization. When the Braves top executive first saw my brother down in the Instructional League, he shouted out, "Where did you find this fat kid?"

As a first baseman myself, I wasn't exactly a speedster on the base paths either. But for Joe Torre, success in professional baseball was a long shot at best. Certainly if someone had told me when he was at the age of 16, 17 or 18 that his career as a player would turn out the way that it did, that he would become an All-Star, a batting champion, an MVP, and then a World Champion manager and sure-fire Hall of Famer (*Joe Torre was enshrined in the Baseball Hall of Fame in 2014*), I would have said they were smoking some foreign substance, if not injecting it directly in their veins.

The fact remains that he was given an opportunity. It is true, that between the 1957 and 1958 seasons, when the Braves looked like they might renege on accepting Joe into the Instructional League, I balked at reporting to camp. When Joe got the chance, he made the most of it. He was given the opportunity to toughen up, to play the game, and to prove that he could perform. He developed a hell of a lot more rapidly than I or anyone else ever dreamed he would.

I don't care what the scouts or anyone else said, nobody, not even Honey Russell, who signed him, could have dreamed that he was going to be such a success.

Yet, it all stemmed from the damn childhood and the really very negative atmosphere that we had in the house. I was determined, just like I was with my own children when I got married, that he would get a chance.

I was tough on Joe but good to him. I never expressed myself so much with words. I wasn't an "I love you" or a huggy type guy. I was always action-oriented and in my brother's case, it took him a long time to realize what I was trying to do for him and why I was treating him the way I did. I needed to jolt him off the course he was on and wake him into seeing the big picture. It's only really been in the last several years that we've gotten quite close and able to understand each other.

While we were never actually estranged, for a lot of years early on he would have preferred not to talk to me. It seemed like every time we were together that I was picking on him. And in his teenage years, when he ballooned out, it was true.

But at the same time, from the Cadets on, my affiliation with the Braves enabled me to get him behind the scenes with a major league club and see the possibilities for himself. He enjoyed the opportunity to be in the clubhouse with the Braves. He went to games, worked out with the club, interacted with people like Henry Aaron and Duke Snider. Not many kids receive those kinds of opportunities. Tough as it was, we still had a brotherly relationship. It was heartfelt, with the best of intentions.

In 1951 when I was playing with the Denver Bears, Joe took the train from New York to Denver, along with my sister, an aunt and a cousin. They spent three or four weeks of the season there. That's when Joe first had the chance to work out on the field with the ball club.

There's a picture from that era with Joe in a uniform. That's also when he started to balloon up. He's always had to watch his weight. He got really heavy on that trip to Denver.

I guess that was my fault. As teammates and family, we always went to the same diner, Richard's, sometimes a few times a day. Joe was eating three steaks a day. But we were hanging out together, driving to the park, and on one level getting along fine. At the same time, I was giving him a hard time about his weight.

See, that's me. Action speaks louder than words. In my own way I was showing him that I cared. But I wasn't hugging him or being physically affectionate. I was always taking care of him, paying attention to him, and trying to look after him.

When I went to the big leagues, Joe also came out to Milwaukee and visited me. When he got off the plane, I think he was about 15 years old, he was wide-eyed and in awe.

I was able to give him a choice of working with my Braves roommate Tommy Ferguson, who was in charge of running the visiting clubhouse, or, I had a pretty young lady who was going to show him the better things around town.

He chose, as he put it, to shine shoes and hang up freshly washed jock straps for Stan Musial, Ernie Banks, Willie Mays, and all the other players. What teenage boy at the time wouldn't? He had an absolute ball. He had to work his tail off though, get up early in the morning, wash, iron, polish, lug, fold, stack, pack, run errands, and unpack.

He just loved being around the players. It put him on the right path and it was great for him. Watching him grow up and become a teenager, even as a fat teenager, I could see that the only thing he ever really wanted to do was to play baseball.

Back home in Brooklyn though, there was more trouble brewing. When my mother and sisters informed me that Joe

Milwaukee Braves' Clubhouse Manager Tommy Ferguson with his arm around Braves Manager Fred Haney, as Henry Aaron makes his way in from right field following pre-game warm-ups.

wanted to go to parochial high school, I didn't believe them. I knew he wasn't much for schooling and just didn't believe that it was his choice. They were all very religious and I felt that my sister, Marguerite, the nun, was putting this pressure on him.

I tried to get him to acknowledge that but they had done such a good job on him that he insisted that he wanted to go to the parochial high school—St. Francis.

That caused a civil war in the house because my father insisted that Joe go to a public school. The old man gave one of his usual ultimatums. Either Joe goes to the local public school, or the old man is going to do something violent in the household. There was a continual threat. This was his way of saying, "Either do it my way or don't do it at all."

This period was also at the beginning of the end—of the family deciding to move the old man out of the house. These were very trying times.

As a young ballplayer, I certainly was not rolling in dough, but I had some means and I told my mother and Joe that if he really wanted to go to the parochial school, I would pay whatever it was.

Dear Old Dad

The Torre sisters, Rae (left) and Sister Marguerite, raise a toast to their brother, New York Yankees skipper, Joe Torre. (Internet)

With my father, partly I think it was an ego thing and the fact that it wasn't his idea. By threatening violence he was saying, "This is my castle and I'm the king." That's the way he was. He wasn't about to pay for it and he didn't want anyone to know that somebody else was paying for his son to go to school. He didn't want anyone upsetting his applecart and he didn't have to have a reason for doing things.

Needless to say, Joe was deathly afraid of my father. Just the old man's presence and the tension that existed when my father was in the house were unbearable, and it just made life miserable for my brother.

But as far as smacking him around was concerned, it just didn't happen. But abusing him verbally happened all the time. It was outrageous the way the cop with the gun was always putting Joe down, even as a small child.

The epitome of it all was the time, and Joe tells this story, when the kid took a loud leak upstairs when there were guests sitting downstairs. The poor kid wasn't older than seven. When he came down the stairs, the old man berated him loudly in front of those people for not closing the door. He was just a little kid. He should have closed the door. It was a small house. And I'm not saying you don't reprimand your son at the proper time and place. But to wait until he walks down the stairs and then make a joke of him at a very young age in front of everybody in the place is not the right thing to do.

That was the kind of treatment Joe received and it created an effect in him. As he grew up, he took greater and greater care to avoid my father in every way.

My sisters and brothers tell me, though, that I was a lot like my father—tough, blunt, no fears. In fact, as I got older, 17, 18 years old, if I knew my father was home, I made a habit of striding boldly into the house, since I knew he wouldn't intimidate or threaten my mother as long as I was around.

There had been incidents, such as with the knife, where I had to stand up to him, on behalf of the family, and he knew I wasn't going to let him get away with the worst of his behavior. He knew I wasn't afraid of him and that I would barge in if I needed to. I had done it before and I would do it again. It didn't disturb me and that's why the whole exercise of me tossing him out unfolded.

It is not a little thing for a family to toss the father out of the house, especially when the old man is a New York City police detective who brandishes weapons. But you have no idea how difficult it was for me playing in the minor leagues in one town after another and getting these terror-stricken late night phone calls from my sister Rae or from my mother. My other sister, Marguerite, was already out of the house and into the cloistered nun's environment.

I would be out on the road, first playing with Denver, then with Hartford, and every day, every week, Rae or my mother would be calling me at home or out on the circuit, and telling me that something had happened that day, or that my father was going to come home that night and kill them all. He threatened it and they believed it.

This was a constant thing, while I'm a thousand, two thousand or two hundred miles away. It stayed in my mind, it stuck in my stomach, on the bus or the train, out on the field, back in my room. There really wasn't anything I could do about it.

Sometimes there would be just a message. Call home. I knew what it was. It could not be good. Usually at the time of night when they would call, I would be home or in a hotel room. It would be after a ball game. My father kept very unpredictable hours.

Whether it was his job, or his other activities, maybe a little bit of both, he left the house in the mid- to late afternoon every day. Unless he was having a card game at the house, he wouldn't come home until the wee hours of the morning, and they never knew what might set him off.

Whatever was eating him, he chalked it up to his job. Giving the benefit of the doubt, maybe it was his job occasionally. Being a cop was tough, even in those days with the extra pay on the side.

Not that he was a drinker. That was the one thing he didn't do. He didn't drink, although sometimes he acted like he did with his wild mood swings and displays of temper.

I think some of those phone calls from my sister or my mother derived from the suspense, the anxiety, the fear of just waiting for him to get there. How could they sleep? It was like a bad dream, or a movie. A real horror show.

They would call me and wake me and I would listen, but I was helpless a thousand miles away. What made it worse was the knowledge that if I had been there, there would have been no real fear.

When I was there, his effect on the house was very subtle. I knew he wouldn't threaten to do anything because I might do it to him instead. I think at that stage of my life, I probably would have. My presence intimidated the old man.

Thinking back on it now, when my father came home, he had a tendency to sit at the dining room table half the time just playing solitaire. It was eerie. This went on when I was a teenager, and I mean a young teenager even before I went on to play ball.

As the older brother, Rocco took a lot of the heat. If I did something wrong, Rocco often was the one who took the blows and got the verbal and physical abuse. He definitely got smacked around a little bit, since it was sort of an unwritten rule that the oldest was responsible.

But I also got the back of the hand and received more than my share of stinging remarks. After a while, my father realized, in spite of his own crudeness and dominant ways that being abusive or being physical with me weren't doing him any good. If anything I'd put out my chin and say, "go ahead hit me again."

He knew I meant it and I never backed down and I couldn't be bribed. While my father was brutish, he was actually very intelligent. Sometimes he'd offer to let you use the car or he would try to give you a few bucks, but I would never accept them. In fact, at times when I was deserving of financial or other reward for certain things, I wouldn't accept it because I didn't want to give him the satisfaction.

He also knew that it disturbed my brother Rocco that he got the worst of it. As a result, he purposely piled it on Rocco even more. That's the kind of antagonist my dad was. After the pro scouts came knocking for Rocco, who was a pretty fine ballplayer himself, and the old man refused to let him sign because he was a minor, Rocco took the first way out and went right into the Navy.

More to intimidate Rocco than me, one of the things my father used to do was take us with him on some of his rougher assignments. Even though he never had any truly high rank in terms of captain or sergeant with the police department, I have been present when judges and police inspectors called him "Joe the boss." That's quite sobering for a kid to hear.

He really was one of the people in charge. He had a great mind and he could go in a lot directions at one time. When he'd get pissed off at my brother and me, he would take us to this restaurant in Brooklyn where he "held court," as we called it, sort of to show us, I guess.

All the people who were running vice or bookmaking were basically standing in line to get permission to operate from my father, and we would see these characters whose pictures had been in the newspapers over the previous month or two. These were the guys with the big cigars and the pinky rings. That's how I became used to the mannerisms and the language of small time hoodlums and everything else.

I know that today there is a lot of sensitivity among the Italian community about the mob, but what we've seen with the Sopranos is pretty much like it was. There was great bonding among certain people and there was a great organization. They used very direct language. My sisters, especially Rae (*Rae Torre passed away in 2015*), resented this stereotyping very much. But really, most of the things that go on with a certain class of Italians are true. I witnessed a lot of exactly what's in *The Sopranos* when I was a kid on the streets of Brooklyn.

I know that my brother Rocco was scared to death of getting sucked into it. (*Rocco Torre died in 1996*).[2] After a while I used to say to myself, "here we go again," even though I was a kid. I don't think it's really insulting, it was just an era within the Italian community. It was how they did business, how they operated. I'm sure that each and every nationality wheeled and dealt in some suspect way once or twice in their lifetimes. I don't think that anybody who is Italian should be embarrassed or angry. With any religion or race, there's good and bad.

In fact, with most people, like in the Sopranos, for every-thing bad that they do, they really are trying their best to avoid the same things in life happening to their kids. They want to pass on a better life to the next generation.

I guess that's why all three of the *Godfather* films were my favorites, because this was reality, these were things that we always saw. (*Often during the taping of his story, Frank had one of the Godfather movies playing in the background. During the interview process, he would stop the tape to watch a favorite scene from one of the movies.*) The men were always of the mind, "This is my castle, and I'm the king." I guess that's why as I grew up, I used to dream that if I ever laid a hand on my kids, the good Lord should burn my fingers, and why I tried to avoid all of the things that I hated happening to me when I was a kid. I went to great extremes to do so.

So in this environment, my father was doing very well, materially, even if he was basically leading two different lives. Put it this way, there was money in it. Without using names or anything, we're in the late thirties, maybe the early forties, and this was the way that it was done.

At times, we had a lot of tin cans in the house with cash in them. While my mother tried to make that $260 stretch, my father went to Florida, gambled, lived a very good life and ate in the best of restaurants. I'm sure his income was pretty substantial in those days.

Then later, out in the minor leagues, as I said, I was getting physically and mentally beat up, getting these calls fairly often in the middle of the night from my sisters and my mother saying, "Dad's going to come home tonight and kill us." I was having one of my worst seasons as a result.

There he was, a policeman and always a gun in the house. And there I was, a thousand or eight hundred miles away, where I couldn't do anything about the whole scene. After that season when I went home for the winter, I had thought it over carefully, and said to my mother, "We either get him out of the house while I'm home now, or when I leave in the spring I'm not coming back. I can't continue putting up with this, or something terrible is going to happen. The only way you're ever going to do it is with me here now. I'm the only one who is not afraid of him. He knows I'm not afraid of him and I'm twice as big as he is. He's not going to mess with you while I'm here, but we have to act. We can't wait."

Indeed, he had pretty much stopped messing with my mother and terrorizing whoever was around with me there, but the knife incident still resonated and he knew I would jump all over him at the slightest provocation if I was around.

This particular time, when I proposed that we team up and make the old man leave, my mother didn't have to think about it too long. She knew what I was saying was true. I probably would not have followed up about not ever coming back, but I had to say something drastic to shake my mother up. Her tendency was always to retreat, even in the face of this malicious treatment. If my sister Rae would even meekly talk back to my father, she'd be shushed up, and thus this truly vicious cycle was never ending.

Rocco and my sister the nun were no longer living with this psychological abuse on a daily basis, but Joe was on the receiving end and I was getting the calls.

Finally, Rae and I went to a lawyer. We were the ones who were going to have to figure out how to pay the bills. My sister the nun couldn't deal with it. Rocco had his own responsibilities, and after leaving the Navy, he now had a young family and was also in the police force.

We instructed the lawyer to put together a very simple legal agreement pretty much stating, "You sign this piece of paper and you will get out of the house. You sign the house over to your wife and with that, you'll not have to pay child support and you'll not have to pay alimony." You're talking maybe five or six thousand dollars as to the value of the house, maybe less. It had to be less, because my mother and father only paid fifty-nine hundred for that house. Whatever was left on it couldn't have been a whole lot of money, but at the time it was considered a bunch.

When the day arrived, Mom, Rae, Joe, and I were there. I think Joe stood in the background. It was very sad. I'm the only one who did any talking and I told him, "Dad, this can't go on. Nobody's happy, so the best thing for everybody is, we want you to get out of the house, and just sign this." He wasn't happy. I don't recall that he even said anything at all. He just looked at all of us. It was a tragic moment. It was a terrible thing for Joe to see. My heart sinks to this day just thinking about it. He didn't want to do it, but he knew he had no choice, so he signed the agreement and got out, that very day.

In the long run, it worked out better for everyone. He knew I was basically the one who kicked him out. I took the brunt, but his life went on and so did ours. He and I stayed in communication, but no one else in the family spoke with him.

Dear Old Dad

Frank as a young lefty pitcher for the Brooklyn Cadets, here sporting a Yankees cap. Frank tossed two victories in two days for the Cadets, helping the club win the national amateur tournament in 1949.

A couple of years later, I actually convinced my brother Joe to talk to him and sort of helped make peace between him and Rocco and my sister the nun. There was some reconciliation among us. My other sister Rae and my mother, however, would never talk to him again. My mother went to her grave and he went to his without any of that happening. To this day, Rae does not have a kind word to say about him.

It came down to a matter of a Florida divorce between my parents. Being very religious, my mother never agreed to what was considered a real divorce.

In the eyes of the Church she was still married, but he was able to marry this girl, Marge, he had been seeing for a number of years. We somehow managed, my sister and I, to pay the bills, even though I really wasn't making that much money then, being still in the minor leagues.

Rae worked for the telephone company where she ended up having a nice career, and my mother used to take in sewing and crocheting, her homework. She worked very hard and times were tough, but without the threats and fear hanging over her head, it was the happiest time of my mother's life.

When my father died, I went to his apartment. Any time any tragedy hit the family, I was now the older brother. My brother Rocco wanted no part of it. I had to go pick up my dad's bankbook and whatever other personal stuff was there. He had the spectacular sum of $200 in the bank.

I'll never forget, his brothers and sisters insisted on seeing all of us, even before we put my father's body out for the wake. Their biggest concern was who was going to pay for the funeral. I said to them almost in disgust, "Rest assured we'll bury him and you won't have to pay anything for it."

I even tossed the so-called "bank-book" at them, although his wife at the time was entitled to it. She got that and whatever other stuff he had there. My mother died about a year after he did.

Because my mother never signed any papers when they split, in the Catholic religion, she had just a separation. But my father got the Florida divorce and married Marge.

My sisters never bothered to tell any of their friends that my mother and father were divorced. For the ten or fifteen years after this Florida divorce, up to the time my mother died, none of our family friends ever knew much about the actual situation.

When my father died, my mother came to me and said, "I want to be at the funeral parlor." I'll go to my grave feeling strongly that my two sisters put her up to it. She hadn't talked to my father for more than ten years, but she was not divorced and this was her husband.

I tried my best to convince her that this was foolish, that it didn't make any sense, but she insisted. I had to go to the funeral parlor people and make special arrangements to get two rooms and put the open coffin with the body in the middle.

You had one room for his current wife, Marge, her side, and one room for our family and friends. It was standing room only in our area and there was nobody in the other room grieving with his current wife. But there was nothing I could do about it and those were the days, and I guess it still exists, where at a funeral parlor, you'd have a daytime session and then a nighttime session.

Now, his wife, Marge, did have a tendency to have a few drinks too many and my older brother, God bless him, was working the back of the room, primarily concerned with the old Italian custom of seeing how much money the mourners gave. They'd have to mark the book up front and he'd check the sign-in book against his own book.

The daytime session was uneventful, except for the tension, and when we came in the evening we were exhausted from going through this emotional wringer. Now my brother Rocco says to me, "We have problems, we have problems." I said, "What do you mean we got problems?" He says, "Well, Marge is carrying on."

In between sessions, she had apparently had a few pops, and so, "You better go over and see her," he tells me. I go over and sit next to her, and she starts whining, "Get her out of here, get her the hell out of here."

I'm trying to act dumb. "What are you talking about, Marge?"

She's moaning, "Get that woman out of here, she doesn't belong here. He's my husband and everybody is giving their condolences to her." Obviously she was referring to my mother.

I just kept trying to be calm. I offered her a mint and said to her, "Marge, if my father would come out of that coffin and speak, he'd just say, 'bury me peacefully.' Why don't you calm down, why don't you just take it easy?"

I kept doing that, but meanwhile I had a splitting headache and I was getting tired of this. Marge knew I was a lot like my father, and I knew he had left my mother and gone to his girlfriend who was now his wife. He continued smacking her around like he used to my mother.

Finally I reached a point where she was getting uncontrollable. I looked her in the eye and said, "You see that coffin up there? If you don't sit here and shut your fucking mouth, I'm going to get another coffin and put you in it." Then I just walked away.

My brother was sitting in the back, puzzled. "What the hell did you say to her? What did you do?" She just clammed up and behaved herself for the rest of the time.

Maybe it wasn't the right thing to do, but I didn't have any choice. Anything milder would not have been effective. It would have become even more embarrassing and she would have made an even bigger scene that wouldn't have benefited anybody. As with previous incidents, I did it to take the pressure off my mother.

One thing for sure, when we put the old man to rest, we also buried a lot of heartache.

The Glory Years

*F*RANK WAS TEARING UP THE MINOR LEAGUES *with both bat and glove and had a clear bead on the major leagues when the Chinese invasion of Korea intervened and the Korean War broke out. Frank's life detoured into a war zone. Frank spent his 20th birthday on a troop ship to Japan en route to Korea and has described landing on bleak, dung-covered Korean soil. He made the most of it though, improving his fielding on the rocky surfaces of the war-torn land and taking charge of a team of misfits that included some officers reluctant to take orders from a kid, and much less run laps, as instructed by a draftee with just a bit of attitude.*

Frank Torre finally joined the big leagues with the Milwau-kee Braves in 1956 after minor league stints from 1951-52 and 1954-1955 with Denver, Hartford, Atlanta and Toledo. He hit .327 in 544 at-bats with AAA Toledo before sticking with the Milwaukee Braves.

My five years with the Braves in the 1950s mirror rather closely the Braves "glory" years. In that fleeting span of time, 1956 to 1960, the club hit the heights and then began a long slow decline. In 1956, we went into the famous "September swoon" and lost the National League crown by a single game. In 1957, we won a World Series in seven games against the Yankees, and in 1958, we lost a World Series, also in seven games, to the same Bronx Bombers. We then came up short again in 1959, losing to the Dodgers in a play-off for the National League pennant. By 1960, the magic was gone. And I had gone from being a raw rookie to a discarded veteran.

Prior to that great run, from the moment the Braves arrived in Milwaukee, they fielded strong clubs. In the years 1953-1955, the Braves finished second in the National League twice and third once. With great depth of talent and a strong farm system, it was only a matter of time before they broke through on top. I was lucky and honored to be a rookie in 1956 when we came close to winning the pennant for the first time.

There are critics, though, who say we should have won four championships. That's hindsight speaking 20/20. There is no doubt, however, that we were nearly a team for the ages, with Hall of Famers like Henry Aaron, Warren Spahn, and Eddie Mathews, and all-time greats like Lew Burdette, Del Crandall, and Johnny Logan, gracing the field at Milwaukee County Stadium. It was a golden time.

"Hammerin' Hank," Henry Aaron, the man who broke Babe Ruth's home run record, rehearses his swing. A power hitter to all fields, he adjusted later in his career to achieve greater home-run production, ending his stellar career with 755 four-base shots and 3,771 hits.

Ed Mathews, power-hitting Milwaukee Braves third baseman. The B on the cap is for Boston. Mathews was the only Braves player to play in Boston, Milwaukee, and Atlanta. He and his mighty swing landed on the first *Sports Illustrated* cover on August 16, 1954.

The amazing Warren Spahn, the winningest left-handed pitcher of all time with 363 wins, his left elbow here at rest.

The slugging Milwaukee Braves first baseman Joe Adcock, whose career was entwined with that of Frank Torre at the position from 1956 to 1960. Adcock's towering blasts set distance records in multiple stadiums, some of which stood as long as the stadiums.

My seasons with the club were particularly linked with Joe Adcock, the huge, power-hitting, slightly flawed-in-the-field first baseman who seemed always to stand in my way. Joe certainly did cast a tall and awesome shadow. At 6 foot 4 and 220 pounds, he was one of the most fearsome sluggers of our day.

I wasn't exactly tiny, at 6 foot 3 and 205, but I was considered a slicker fielding first baseman than Joe. Still, it was my fate frequently to play behind him.

Often, I was thrown in as a substitute for Joe Adcock on defense. More than once I spelled him when he was injured, and the times I got to play the most and really show my stuff, were, sad to say, the times when Joe was hurt—most notably

when he broke his leg early (June 23)[3] in the 1957 campaign.

Frank Torre hit from the left side of the plate. A lifetime .273 hitter, when given the chance to play almost every day, Frank hit .272 and .309 in 1957 and 1958, respectively. He clobbered two home runs in the 1957 World Series. Frank was a league-leading fielder at his first base position.

The Glory Years

I was a rookie in the 1956 campaign and didn't see all that much action. I made appearances in 111 games and only batted 159 times.

The club, while powerful, was new to a true pennant race. With an eight-game lead under our belts in August, we proceeded to do a swan dive that was famous at the time. We ended up falling a game short of winning the pennant and Brooklyn went on to lose to the Yankees in the World Series that year.

In 1957, however, when Adcock broke his leg, I became the regular first baseman. I hit well, was the top fielding first baseman in the National League (Gil Hodges won the Gold Glove, although I had a slightly better fielding percentage) and the Braves became the champions in seven games.

In 1958, Adcock and I platooned at the position, with me getting most of the starting nods. Joe was not pleased with the situation, but I played a lot, hit .309 for the year and won another top fielding first baseman's award. In the 1958 World Series, after jumping to a commanding 3-1 lead over the

The incomparable Gil Hodges, Brooklyn and Los Angeles Dodgers first baseman, well-recorded in history, just not in the Baseball Hall of Fame. Hodges garnered Gold Gloves defending first base in 1957, 1958 and 1959, the very years Torre was gracing the diamond with slightly higher fielding percentages.

Yankees, we lost the final two games at home and fell to the Yankees four games to three.

In 1959, in a see-saw finish to a fine regular season, the Braves went into a best of three games play-off against the Dodgers for the National League pennant, and dropped the series 2-0.

The next year, 1960, the Braves finished 88-66, but fell seven games behind the Pirates and their star Roberto Clemente, and I got sent down to Louisville somewhere around midseason. Milwaukee attendance slipped to under a million and a half at the gate, only fourth best in the National League, and the thrill was gone.

While the Braves remained competitive and struggled for a few more years in Milwaukee, it wasn't long before the team's owners broke the city's collective heart and shipped the club to Atlanta for the 1966 season—but only after a bitter court battle kept them in Milwaukee for an anticlimactic 1965.[4]

Pittsburgh Pirates right-fielder Roberto Clemente bursts out of the batter's box. Clemente won four National League batting titles and was league Most Valuable Player in 1966.

It was a great time to be a Brave and a Milwaukeean. As club owners, the Perini brothers Lou (left) and Charles flank Milwaukee Mayor Frank Zeidler (dark coat) and the first Milwaukee Braves Manager, Charlie Grimm (in hat, arms extended.)[5]

The Braves' glory years of the 1950s were a tremendous time and I was privileged to be a part of them. No matter what anyone says, no city has ever thrilled to a baseball Renaissance like Milwaukee did—not Los Angeles, not New York, not San Francisco.

For decades in the 1930s and '40s, Milwaukee was a fine minor league town with the old, original Brewers. In 1953, when the Braves moved from Boston to Milwaukee, the town went truly bonkers. Through 1958, the club established major league attendance records, pulling in more than two million fans four years straight.[6]

Milwaukee had really set the world of baseball on its ear. In those days, a line shot single in Milwaukee by a utility infielder in the month of May reverberated through the grandstands like a play-off homerun anywhere else. People went nuts on loud foul balls.

Put it this way, if the Braves don't happen in Milwaukee, the Giants and Dodgers might still be in New York. It was owner jealousy, and greed over the success of the Braves that caused both New York clubs to head west for presumably greener pastures.

In those few, short, fast years, I played with and against some of the greatest ballplayers ever to step onto the field. My teammates and friends included Warren Spahn, Henry Aaron, Eddie Mathews, Lew Burdette, Don McMahon, Bill Bruton, Red Schoendienst, Wes Covington and Johnny Logan. I played against greats like Willie Mays, Jackie Robinson, Mickey Mantle, Whitey Ford, Ernie Banks, Gil Hodges, Duke Snider, Yogi Berra, Don Larsen, Roberto Clemente, Orlando Cepeda, Frank Robinson, and Stan Musial.

The truly fleet-footed center fielder Bill Bruton, mainstay of the dynamic teams of the 1950s, hit the first home run in Milwaukee County Stadium, against the Cardinals to win the game 3-2 in the tenth inning, April 14, 1953.

True greats convene: Hall of Famers Yogi Berra, New York Yankees catcher, and Stan Musial, St. Louis Cardinals marvel (OF, 1B), banter in the spring-training sun.

I swung the bat against pitchers like Don Drysdale, Johnny Podres, Robin Roberts, Don Newcomb, Larsen and Ford, Bob Turley, Bob Friend, Sandy Koufax, Sal Maglie, and Hoyt Wilhelm. Oh, yeah, when I later became a Phillie, it was weird playing against some of my former Braves teammates.

I also knew well as a player and as a friend one of the grand broadcasting voices of the game, Bob Uecker. Let's get this out in the open right away. Bob Uecker is one of my great friends, I'm not ashamed to know him, and not only is he a Hall of Fame announcer, without a doubt, he's the best comedian to come out of baseball.

During those heady years of the 1950s, I witnessed or participated in some of the great moments in sport—Henry Aaron's line-shot homerun that won the pennant for the Braves

Sandy Koufax flashed across the major league sky like a meteor of greatness, performing in only 12 big league seasons. Brought up at 19 with the Brooklyn Dodgers in 1955, and making the trip west with the Dodgers in 1958, he was out of baseball by age 30. Posting 165 wins and 87 losses overall he struck out 2,396 batters and recorded a lifetime 2.67 earned run average, 0.95 in post-season play. A seven-time All-Star and three-time Cy Young Award winner, Koufax appeared with the Dodgers in five World Series, winning three championships. The Hall of Famer was the National League's Most Valuable Player in 1963, and World Series MVP in 1963 and 1965. He led the league in ERA five times and strikeouts four times.

in 1957; Lew Burdette's three pitching victories and two shut-out games in the 1957 World Series; Nippy Jones' famous shoe polish incident in the '57 Series; the time four of my team-mates—Aaron, Mathews, Adcock, and Crandall—belted back to back homeruns; and the time Harvey Haddix of the Pittsburgh Pirates lost to the Braves in the 13th inning after pitching 12 perfect innings.

I set a record or two myself, and experienced the highest of highs and the lowest of lows. You'll find my name tied with a few others for scoring the most runs, six, in a single game. I hit two home runs in the 1957 World Series that the Braves won, and took fielding honors at my position in consecutive years. I also get pegged for two controversial (at least according to me) errors in game seven of the 1958 World Series that we lost in heartbreaking fashion.

Frank Torre was thrilled to be breaking into the major leagues as a Milwaukee Brave.

For the historical record, I think I had an advantageous viewpoint of the Braves' greatest seasons. More than half of my perspective comes from being on the field and the rest from a spot in the shade of the dugout. Through every pitch and every inning, I tried to be a student of the game. I think this perspective has helped me over the years in my conversations with my brother Joe, as he's climbed to almost unbelievable heights with the New York Yankees. I think in some small way my mentorship of Joe has helped him achieve his great record.

1956 and the September Swoon

Looking back, it seems less like a dream than it was a very bright chapter in a hard-fought life. In 1956, for the second spring in a row, I was asked to report to the Braves' training camp in Bradenton, Florida. In 1955, when the big boys packed up to start the season, I was headed back to the minors, to Toledo (AAA Sox), where I pounded out a .327 batting average in 544 at-bats with 178 hits for the year.

This time I was hoping to stick with the club when we went north. When I arrived at camp, there was quite a logjam around first base. Charlie Grimm was the manager and between the incumbent, Adcock, another muscular hitter named George Crowe, and myself, there was tough competition for the position.

Luckily for me, Charlie made the decision that Crowe and Adcock were very similar players. Each possessed great offensive skill and was decent defensively. Grimm wanted to change the look, I guess. I played better defense than either of the other guys and he felt that I could hold my own with the bat.

In addition to Adcock, this was also a club that boasted Mathews, Aaron, Covington, Crandall and Bruton at the plate, so there was plenty of firepower. I strengthened us defensively in the infield.

Grimm made the move and traded Crowe to Cincinnati, giving me an opportunity to stick with the club. The trade was significant because George was a veteran Brave who'd been with the team in Boston. He went on to have fine seasons with the Reds and the Cards. The Braves also picked up a prospect named Bob Hazle in the deal. Just a year later, he'd play a huge role in the Braves' success.

Charlie Grimm, legendary player and manager, took the Chicago Cubs to three World Series, and set the Braves up for success in 1956, handing the baton to Fred Haney early that season.

Frank Torre found George Crowe, along with Joe Adcock, crowding the first base position when he joined the club in 1956. Crowe, a Boston Brave who made the trip to Milwaukee, was shortly sent to Cincinnati, where he posted strong numbers in seasons to follow. The trade opened a path to playing time for the young Torre.

My first year up in Milwaukee, 1956, I basically caddied for Adcock. I played in more than 100 games, but I didn't bat much because I was usually a late inning defensive replacement.

From a very early age I had always been the type of person who knew how to play every aspect of the game and paid attention to the nuances on the field. At each level—high school, amateur, semi-pro, the military, the minors—I always used my head. As a youth, I often stood out on the basis of my talent, but when I got into pro ball, everybody had talent and I had to have an opportunity to grow on you, day in and day out. I learned to do all the things that added up. I could bunt, I could hit the ball the other way, and I rarely struck out (64 strike-outs in seven seasons). I was very good in the field.

But I was not a slugger and I was not a speedster. Scouts or coaches were not going to be impressed just watching me play one or two days. I was the kind of player who needed to play day-in, day-out, week-in, week-out to have an impact and be noticed as a valuable person on the ball club. 1956 was not like that for me.

Joe Adcock was whacking the hell out of the ball (.291 for the year with 38 home runs and 103 RBIs) and I came in to clean up and play defense in the late innings. But I was a rookie on one of the best teams in baseball and more than willing to pick my spots.

There were spells when Joe only started against a left-handed pitcher. I batted from the left side of the plate. But he got by far the lion's share of the starts, and deservedly so. He was a Dodger killer, setting a record at the time with 13 home runs in the season against the Bums. In June, he blasted three of those 13 in a double-header at Ebbets field.

An eager, young Frank Torre emerges from the dugout looking to take his cuts.

In the first game of the twin bill, his game-winning shot cleared the 38-foot wall in left and landed on the 83-foot-high roof,[7] the first and only time a hitter ever planted a pitch up there. Joe wound up the season second in the league in both home runs and RBIs, with 38 and 103 respectively, and never again clobbered so many dingers in a single season.

That year, 1956, many picked the Braves to take the National League pennant. Yet after only 46 games, we were languishing back in third place. We didn't seem able to put it all together.

As a consequence, club ownership lost patience with the venerable Charlie Grimm and replaced him with Fred Haney as manager. To put the move in perspective, Charlie, in some 13 seasons managing the Cubs, had a solid winning record and took Chicago to three World Series, winning three pennants. He'd managed the Braves since their arrival from Boston and had several fine seasons, but I guess the owners felt Charlie would almost go all the way again, and that was not their plan.

Frankly, Charlie had lost control of the club. As great a guy as he was, he wasn't tough enough for the boisterous young crew. There were quite a few jokesters on the club, including Spahn and Burdette. Jack Dittmer, our left-hand hitting second baseman, was the class clown. He did things like crawl under the bench and tie Charlie's shoelaces together or light them on fire.

Charlie would go out to change the pitcher and there'd be smoke coming from his feet and his shoelaces were on fire. Or Dittmer would find people day-dreaming in the dugout and give them a hot foot. You've always got a little of that going on (see Uecker, Bob), some of it good, but sometimes the timing was detrimental to the team effort, and it reinforced general patterns of disrespect in the clubhouse.

Milwaukee Braves Manager Fred Haney replaced Charlie Grimm as Braves pilot early in the 1956 season and guided the powerful club to two World Series and a National League Pennant play-off. Haney's Braves suffered a famous September Swoon in 1956, just missing the NL pennant, and lost a play-off for the pennant in 1959. The Milwaukee Braves under Haney won the World Series in 1957, defeating the New York Yankees, and lost it to the Yankees after leading three games to one in 1958.

Haney was different and commanded respect. He put some of our jokers like Spahn and Burdette in line, sometimes with just a look. Dittmer wasn't around for more than another year. Everybody knew our mission was to win a championship and pretty soon everybody got with the program. Almost immediately under Haney, we went on a tear and won 11 straight games, vaulting back into contention. Within a month we were in first place.

Heading into the month of August, we were the team to beat. Everything was going our way until an 11 win–12 loss season closing stretch proved too much for us to overcome. Maybe the bell was tolling for us late in August during that mediocre run when Cincinnati touched up our pitching staff for eight home runs in a single game. Perhaps it was George Crowe's revenge.

Jackie Dittmer, plucky second baseman and occasional cut-up.

We had a slight lead on the Dodgers early in September but mid-month they beat us and pulled even at the top of the National League standings. We took a single game lead with three to play into St. Louis to play the Cardinals the last weekend of the season. To make a sad story short, we dropped the first two games in St. Louis as the Dodgers won their two, giving them a one-game lead, and even though we won on Sunday, so did the Dodgers.

Those first two games were particularly frustrating for all of us. We had men all over the bases while Bobby Del Greco, the center fielder for the Cardinals roamed the outfield making one sensational catch after another. This was true the entire series. In one instance, the Braves' Dittmer, who wasn't known for his power, hit a bullet to right centerfield that should have been out of the reach of anybody, but somehow, some way, Del

Bobby Thomson replicates his "Shot Heard 'Round the World." Into the history books forever with his dramatic pennant winning home run for the Giants to beat the Dodgers and win the National League pennant on October 3, 1951 (in the first ever nationally televised baseball game), Thomson was a Milwaukee Brave from 1954 until one-third into the 1957 season. A three-time All-Star, his best year was 1949 when he batted .309 and hit 25 home-runs. He led the National League in triples with 14 in 1952. Thomson was a life-time .271 hitter with 259 home runs and 1,006 runs-batted-in in 15 major league seasons.

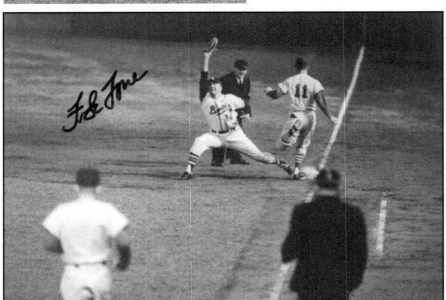

Frank Torre fully extends his 6 foot 3 frame to record a bang-bang out at first base. Frank led the league in fielding his position in 1957 and 1958.

Greco was off at the crack of the bat and there were a couple of men on and he made a sensational catch.

A couple of different times Bobby Thomson came to bat with men on first and second and no one out. (*Bobby was the legendary hero of the Giants win over the Dodgers on October 3, 1951, when he hit a jaw-dropping home run down the line in the ninth inning to win the pennant, so there were very high hopes for him each time he came to the plate.*) He had chances to bunt men over to get us in scoring position, but both times he fouled out, once into a double play. In one of those losses, Spahn pitches for us and wasn't bad. He kept people off base, and he was going through one inning after another. But the hitters never got the job done. Even though we won the final game of the season, we finished in second place with a 92 and 62 record, a game behind Brooklyn.

Just to rub it in, early the next season in Chicago, where Del Greco was traded, somebody hit a lazy pop-up to Bobby in center field, and he dropped it. The entire Braves dugout groaned.

Sure we were mightily disappointed with how 1956 ended, but this was primarily a young club. We had stumbled in the stretch. It was our first taste of how tough it is to break through and close it out at the top. The good folks of Milwaukee were not pleased, however, and our stumble near the end became widely known as the "September swoon."

Milwaukee fans had come out in droves and attendance topped two million. It was widely acknowledged by then that these were the best fans in baseball, however you defined "best."

I had made a credible showing in my first year in the big leagues. I hadn't exactly stormed the league with my bat, but in 111 game appearances and some 160 (159) at bats I hit .241,

Pinch-hitting left-fielder Chuck Tanner, armed and dangerous, at Milwaukee County Stadium.

The versatile Danny O'Connell played every infield position over his 10-year major league career. He was traded away for Red Schoendienst early in 1957.

(*Frank's average was .258*) and struck out four times. With his 38 home runs, more than 100 RBIs and a .291 batting average, Adcock struck out about 90 times, and really put his name in lights.

Henry Aaron led the club batting .328. Ed Mathews hit 37 home runs. The Braves' pitching was excellent, with Spahn picking up his 20 wins, Burdette, 19, and Bob Buhl, 18.

There was a great contributing cast, including Danny O'Connell, a feisty second baseman, and Chuck Tanner, who went on to become a great manager.

What a thrill it was for me, a 26-year-old rookie, to be playing in the big leagues against players like Jackie Robinson and Stan Musial. Take that crazy final weekend of play. While Robinson is starring for the Dodgers on one coast, we're playing

In a notorious imbroglio, usually congenial but intensely competitive Roy Campanella got into a wild argument with the umps, was restrained on all sides, and ejected from the game. Campy won three MVP awards and hit .312 with 142 RBIs in 1953.

Musial and the Cardinals in the Heartland. It was quite a cast of characters.

My rookie year was Jackie Robinson's last, and his numbers were down a bit, but what an honor to be on the same field. Jackie Robinson undoubtedly was the most exciting base runner I'd ever seen, even though he wasn't the fastest. Other guys stole more bases, but the two things about Jackie Robinson were, number one, when he got on first base, he could take a lead where guys like Warren Spahn, who had great moves, and would throw over there, sure to pick him off, couldn't touch him. He would always get back. And when you would get lucky and get Jackie in a pickle between bases, I have never seen a person who could stay in the pickle (that's what we called it in those days) for as long as he did and more times than not get out of it.

He was elusive, quick and would evade the tag. He would stop on a dime and go back and forth, and would drive you absolutely crazy. An amazing guy. He just had such a great feel for the game and this ferocious competitive willpower.

Stan Musial was probably one of the most natural hitters ever. He could hit coming out of bed. I remember when the Dodgers moved from Ebbets Field to the Coliseum. Stan was basically a pull hitter, but he also moved the ball around the field. Ebbets Field was a dream for left-handed hitters because you had the short right field, short right center, and Musial used to go crazy there.

The normally mild-mannered Campy carried his beef into the dugout where he continued the tirade tossing towels and anything else he could get his hands on onto the field of play. Here we see the fiery but always contained Jackie Robinson (42) urging his teammate to cease and desist so he can bat.

Then when the Dodgers moved to the Coliseum, the observers said, "Boy, Stan's in a lot of trouble because right field's 450 feet away." I believe the first game he played at the Coliseum he hit four balls off the short fence in left field. He just adjusted and went the other way. He was a .350 hitter (*in five of his 20 All-Star seasons*) and he didn't run badly, but he wasn't a speedster so he didn't get that many leg hits. He got base hits. Lefties didn't daunt him either. It was a classic match-up watching Warren Spahn trying to get him out. He didn't do too well at it. Stan hit Warren well.

As astute as I was, my rookie year was a great education. Pee Wee Reese took me to the cleaners once, and I never forgot the lesson. Pee Wee was a great base runner but he wasn't fast afoot. He would take extreme leads and it was almost like he had an innate instinct. He knew when the pitcher was going to throw over and he'd just get back. Even though he wasn't speedy, he could steal a base anytime he wanted. He was a thinking man's player.

Stan Musial steps into a line drive. Stan the Man posted a .331 lifetime batting average over 22 seasons, winning three MVP awards.

This one time we had Pee Wee picked off first base and in a run down and I was just a rookie. Of course, there are certain rules and regulations. On defense you can't get in the way of the runner. On offense, you have to stay in the base-path. We had him pickled and I threw to the second baseman and stepped onto the grass getting out of the way because now somebody behind me was going to cover.

Pee Wee, being the brain that he was, intentionally ran me deeper into the grass. With me being a rookie and he being Pee Wee Reese, the umpire called interference on me.

Until the day he died, Pee Wee told the story about how he tricked me. Even as he got awarded the base, he had a shit-eating grin on his face, as if to say, "Kid, you're dealing with 'the Colonel,'" as everybody called him. It was about 30 years before I got him back.

Harold Henry "Pee Wee" Reese, the Little Colonel, played 16 seasons for the Dodgers, with only his final year (1958) in Los Angeles. He was a ten-time All Star at shortstop representing the Brooklyn club, leading the league in runs scored once, stolen bases once, and bases on balls once. The Hall of Famer appeared in seven World Series, losing to the Yankees six times and taking the crown in 1955. He racked up 46 World Series hits, scoring 20 times, driving in 16 runs, and posting a .272 post-season batting average. Reese was known for his strong support of Jackie Robinson in the latter's early years in major league baseball, and after hanging up his glove, Pee Wee enjoyed a career as a play-by-play announcer.

1957: World Series Champions

Some of us licked our wounds after falling a game short in 1956, by hibernating in the sub-zero Milwaukee weather, while others went south for the winter. Some of us did both. But in the spring of 1957, we were like kids out there at our Bradenton, Florida spring training camp. There is hope for the worst teams at spring training and we were among the best. We knew we could go over the top this year. There was an air of breezy confidence, and it was FUN to be a Milwaukee Brave.

For the 1957 season, my salary jumped to $8,000. John Quinn, the general manager, sold it to me as a one-third raise. He didn't add that the minimum salary in the big leagues had gone up in the off-season from $6,000 to $8,000. He was basically giving me ice in the wintertime. If I was in the big leagues, he had to pay me $8,000. I should have pushed back and asked for more, but you have to understand, you were glad to be there.

I went to spring training and since we had been reasonably successful the year before, I was again going to have to just pick my spots. It looked like I was going to play the same role, but Haney was more into using his whole team than Grimm had been, and therefore I might get to play a little more in Haney's first full season.

While I was used to carrying Joe Adcock's luggage, we were friends and I looked up to him. That spring and during most of our competitive days, we were both single guys. Joe always used to complain to me that I had all these pretty women and why didn't I fix him up with a girl and all this kind of stuff. At the time, I was dating a water skier in Winter Haven.

In spring training, we had an exhibition game in Fort Myers, and nobody ever wanted to take the trip from Bradenton to Fort Myers. Only one team trained there and at the time it was the Pirates. Bradenton to Fort Myers was a long jaunt. The bus had to leave about six in the morning just to play the game.

Before I made a date to go see this girl in Winter Haven, which also was a good distance from Bradenton, I made sure I wasn't on the list for the trip to Fort Myers. I looked at who was on the traveling team and saw that I wasn't going to play against the Pirates the next day, Adcock was. Adcock knew I was dating this water skier and he asks me, "Why don't you see if she's got a girlfriend?"

I said, "Hell Joe, you've got to make the trip to Fort Myers. You've got to get up early."

Milwaukee Braves slugging first baseman Joe Adcock famously hit for power and distance. On July 31, 1954, he hit four home runs and a double, setting a record for most total bases (18) in a single game that stood until 2002. He also hit the famous non-home run that sent Felix Mantilla across home plate for the Braves to defeat the Pittsburgh Pirates in Harvey Haddix's previously perfect game in the 13th inning. After Felix Mantilla scored, Henry Aaron thought Adcock had hit a double and walked off the infield, causing Adcock to pass him on the bases. Adcock was ruled out and his homer nullified and determined to be a double, but Haddix and the Pirates had lost the game 1-0. Joe hit 336 home runs in a 17-year big league career, and was a 1960 All-Star.

Then he says, "Oh, that's okay, I'll be alright." He really puts the squeeze on me. So I called up the young lady and she fixed Joe up with one of her girlfriends.

We drove over to Winter Haven in a new little Pontiac, a blue job I had. Neither Joe nor I drank very much. When Joe did have a drink, it would usually be beer, but I just couldn't stomach the stuff.

We went out on the date, and Joe had about two or three beers during the evening, not anything spectacular, but the two or three beers were too much for him.

As we were driving back after midnight, he was hanging out the window and vomiting all over the side of my car, sicker than a dog, all because of two or three beers, and this is the guy known for his towering 500-foot home runs. He was fouling the outside of my brand-new car and I was livid, but I knew it was better than Joe puking all over the inside of my new car.

Then we finally get back and sneak into the Manatee River Hotel, where the players stayed that particular year. I think it's an old-age home now in Bradenton. The next morning about five a.m., I get a phone call. It's only been about three hours from the point where we snuck in. On the phone was our trainer informing me that I was making the trip to Fort Myers because Joe Adcock had come down with the flu. Needless to say, I never fixed up Joe with a woman again.

1957 was the year it all came together for the town and the club. Despite our swoon the previous fall, excitement in the old beer burgh was at a fever pitch and this year we were expected to win.

For the players, the times could not have been better. We were the toast of the town, and although we were well-paid athletes for the time, the town merchants were extremely generous in bestowing us with free goods and services of all kinds.

That's how badly Milwaukee wanted us to win. If they could make our lives easier or cheaper, we didn't even have to ask. They gave. We received free cases of beer and liquor, cars from the area's new car dealers, movie passes, groceries, and even free dry cleaning and laundry service from a nice chain called Spic and Span.

At one point, the owner of the dry cleaner addressed the club in the locker room. Here he was kindly offering 25 players and another dozen or so coaches and staff all his services entirely for free. He started out saying how thrilled Spic and Span was to be part of the Braves winning team. He said Spic and Span was delighted to be successful enough to be in a position to take in all the players' and their families' laundry and clean it all for free.

He said he hoped the players appreciated the quick turnaround for the free service and that all his people were polite at all times.

Milwaukee Braves General Manager John Quinn, whose father also had been a Braves GM, ran the baseball business side of the club from 1946 to 1958. He went on to become the Phillies GM from 1959 to 1972. A Boston College graduate, he started out as a ticket-taker and grounds-keeper, before becoming club secretary (1936-1946).[8]

Not much made Frank happier than being asked to grab a bat for a plate appearance, except perhaps making a smooth put-out at first base.

But there was one little thing, he said, and he took out a stack of receipts and noted that the bills of our power-hitting left fielder Wes Covington were more than all the bills for the entire rest of the team, and he wondered if there was some problem.

Well, it turned out that Wes was scooping up the laundry for his entire extended family, probably everybody he knew in his apartment building, and maybe everybody else he knew in town. The nice man from Spic and Span said that unless that sort of activity was corrected, he wouldn't be able to continue offering the Braves the service.

Needless to say, we all turned on Wes with a vengeance, throwing jocks and towels and stuff at him, because we wanted to protect our free service, and he was quite embarrassed about the whole thing.

Laundry was great, but cars were even better. In fact, there was real competition among the car dealers to give us free vehicles. Wally Rank was a Dodge dealer in Milwaukee, and a

Milwaukee auto dealer Wally Rank hands out auto maintenance booklets to Braves players who will drive Rank's Buicks. Frank Torre (fourth from right) awaits his gift car standing between Del Crandall and Lew Burdette with Andy Pafko and Red Schoendienst hovering over Rank's left shoulder and Gene Conley, Don McMahon, Warren Spahn and Bob Buhl ranging in from the right, new vehicles arrayed behind them.

dear friend to a lot of the ball players. He supplied all the players with new Dodges and we were more than happy to have them.

Meanwhile, our pitcher Don McMahon became very friendly with a young man named Bud Selig, son of Ben Selig, owner of Knippel-Selig Ford. Bud worked on the lot and in the showroom from time to time as a salesman, selling cars and learning his father's business from the ground up.

Don was driving a Ford from Ben. I got to know Buddy and we got friendly. As we all now know, Bud was a baseball fanatic, and I too started driving a Ford.

Before long, we were holed up in Ben's office, playing cards. Ben loved to play gin and so did I and he was a very pleasant guy. Every once in a while, I would wander over early in the day to Knippel-Selig Ford for a game of cards. Buddy was a mediocre salesman, but he was working hard selling cars right out on the floor. As soon as I showed up, Ben would tell his secretary, "I'm in conference, I don't want to be disturbed," and we'd sit in there and play gin for hours.

Mr. and Mrs. Ben Selig out on the Milwaukee social circuit.

A young Bud Selig and renowned Milwaukee sportswriter Lou Chapman cross paths on the road.

Writer Lou Chapman follows the story as Ben Selig drinks it in.

Below: Bud Selig and friend beneath the stands.

Every now and then, Buddy would get lucky and sell a car, but the procedure was that to finalize the sale, it had to be initialed by the big boss and the big boss was his father. Buddy would be parading up and down outside his father's office going crazy, knowing that we were just playing gin rummy in there and that he couldn't go through that door.

When I'd come out, Bud would make some of his usually raspy comments about wasting his valuable time. Ben was such a competitor and I was a pretty good gin player, so until he won a game, he wouldn't quit. So eventually, I would have to sort of ease up on him to get the game over with and let Bud sell a car.

Who knew that kid would become the savior of baseball in Milwaukee with the Brewers, and then later rise to be the commissioner of Major League Baseball?

One day, I received a new black Thunderbird from Knippel-Selig Ford. I remember the day vividly because I was living over on Prospect Avenue near Lake Michigan in Milwaukee, and it was a beautiful day outside.

I had just picked up a ton of dry cleaning from Spic and Span, and I had a lovely young lady in the car with me. We decided to just pull over by the lake and sit there and talk for a while. This was broad daylight, so I parked the car and we were there for just a few minutes when a truck pulls up next to me and starts blowing the horn and the guy hollers out, "Your hood is on fire, your hood is on fire."

Here I was in a car that had only 15 miles on it and, of course, initially I didn't believe the guy, but then I looked up and saw flames and smoke coming up from around the hood. I hollered for the young lady to get out of the car—and make sure she grabbed my dry cleaning—as I ran around to the hood of the car.

I didn't know what to do because I am not mechanically inclined, but I opened the hood and that only made the flames worse. We just stood there and watched the car burn.

Somebody called the fire department and pretty soon a fire truck pulled up. When the firemen got through putting their foam and water all over the car, it really looked worse. Between the fire and the foam, the car was almost a skeleton when they got through with it.

I was pretty close to home so we walked over to my apartment. I got on the phone and dialed up Bud Selig. "Buddy, I hate to tell you this, but you know, you have a little problem with this car and it's sitting over on Lake Shore Drive near the lake and it's all burned up."

Because we were always playing jokes on each other, he says, "Frank, will you stop kidding me?" He basically walked away from the phone. I had to call back and eventually one of his guys got on the phone. He took me seriously and they sent somebody over to pick up the car.

About a half hour later, I got this screaming return phone call from Buddy, hollering, "What the hell did you do to the car?" Of course, I took the offensive and told him I was going to sue him for giving me defective products and everything else. It must have been faulty wiring.

Well, in 1957, the Milwaukee Braves did have a hell of a team and we had things clicking on all cylinders. You can't discuss that year without talking about the great trio of Aaron, Spahn, and Mathews, and you have to throw in Lew Burdette too.

Henry was the league MVP, batting .322, and led the league with 44 home runs and 132 runs batted in. Spahnnie won the Cy Young award with a 21–11 record and a 2.69 earned run average. Eddie hit .292 and 32 home runs.

It was a great time to be a Brave, as Ty Cobb (in white hat) along with Duffy Lewis (Boston Braves and New York Yankees) and George McBride (right, Pirate, Cardinal, Senator) stop by the Braves clubhouse to wish Fred Haney and the team well and soak up the exciting atmosphere.

The Glory Years

1957 truly was the year that Henry Aaron became the Braves team leader and a great star. From 1953 through 1956, Mathews had been the clear offensive leader. But in our championship year, Henry stepped to the fore in every respect.

Henry Aaron was so talented, it seemed he could do whatever he chose to do. He also worked extremely hard at it. There were certain pitchers, for instance, who were tougher for him to hit, and the Dodgers' Don Drysdale seemed to really have Henry's number. Don threw hard, but not as hard as it appeared. He had this sling shot type of delivery that made it tough to pick up the ball out of his hand and it seemed Hank couldn't hit Drysdale with a tennis racket. He really made Hank look bad up at the plate and Aaron did not like it one bit.

One day, Henry, like only he could do, came back into the dugout after one of his futile at bats against Drysdale, shaking his head and said, "I'm sick and tired of him making a fool of me. From here on in, he's going to know that I was up there."

Well, we were all very curious as to how he was going to do it. But whatever adjustments he made, Henry hit about .500 against Drysdale after that; it seemed by sheer force of will and concentration.

Johnny Podres of the Dodgers also used to make Henry look foolish with one straight change up after another. Henry would always be way out in front of his pitches.

One time, Henry got a straight change that he was so anxious to hit, he hit the ball out of the park—except he was called out because he ran up on the pitch and right out of the batter's box with the swing.

This one particular night, we were playing in the Coliseum, and the first time up, Podres threw one fast ball, strike one, two fast balls, strike two, three fast balls, strike three, and Aaron didn't even swing the bat.

Hank came back to the dugout and I said, "I've never seen you do that, Henry."

He said, "Don't worry, I'll get him."

Well, he had made up his mind, he didn't say anything, but he was going to look only for the changes. Of course, John had a great change-up and it was just a matter of time before he threw it.

When Henry came up again, Podres threw Henry a straight change. The ball was about a foot over Hank's head, but he hit it about a hundred rows up into the stands in left field. When he went up there with a purpose, he was going to punish the pitcher.

Red Schoendienst also came over to the Braves from the Giants about a third through the season and led the league in hits in 1957 with an even 200, two more than Henry, and batted .309 for the year. If you look at the numbers, 1957 was Red's all-time best year at the plate. His 200 hits that year bested Uecker's career total by 54.

Henry Aaron takes a cut against the Phillies, exerting his famous keen wrist action. Aaron was known, along with several others (notably Ernie Banks and Roberto Clemente) for creating powerful pops off the bat with his mighty wrists during the swing.

A dashing Henry Aaron holds his plaque as 1957 National League Most Valuable Player. With 44 homeruns, a .322 batting average, 118 runs scored, 198 hits, and 132 RBIs, Aaron received nine first-place votes to five for Stan Musial, who placed second in the balloting, and batted .351. Milwaukee's Red Schoendienst placed third in the NL-MVP race, and actually received more first-place votes, eight, than his former Cardinal protégé Musial. Warren Spahn placed fifth with one first-place vote based on his 21 win 11 loss, 2.69 season. Ed Mathews placed eighth in the balloting, behind Willie Mays (4th), Ernie Banks (6th) and Gil Hodges (7th).

While Eddie Mathews didn't have his best year in 1957 (*he won the NL homerun crown*), he was one of the toughest individuals both physically and mentally that I have every run into. He was a great competitor.

When Eddie first came up, he was an awful fielder, very crude, very rough, and not polished at all with the glove, but he was a fighter and worked his tail off. There were times in practice where Eddie took one ball after another off his chest. He was close to being a Gold Glove fielder by the time his career ended (*lifetime .956 fielding percentage at the hot corner*).

One time we were playing the Reds in the first game of a doubleheader. We had a tremendous rivalry with the Reds, but we'd always beat their tails off. They had a good team, Birdie Tebbetts was their manager, and the great Frank Robinson was one of their stars. They had Ted Kluszewski, Johnny Temple, Don Hoak, and George Crowe was there now, too.

Ed Mathews lines up his powerful swing. He was a nine time National League All-Star and finished second in MVP balloting in 1959, one of two years in which he led the league in home runs, with 46 (47 in 1953), 182 hits and 114 RBIs. Given his power, Mathews led the league in walks in four different seasons. He wound down his career with one season in Houston and two in Detroit, recording 19 of his 512 career home runs with those two clubs.

Frank Robinson was major league baseball's first African-American manager, here with the San Francisco Giants, and managed five different big league clubs. As a player he hit 586 home runs in 22 seasons and was twice selected National League Most Valuable Player. Rookie of the Year in the first of his ten seasons with Cincinnati, and a World Series Champion twice with the Baltimore Orioles, he was Series MVP in 1966. He is considered one of the greatest right fielders of all time, with a legendary arm. Hall of Famer Robinson led the league in slugging four times and on-base percentage twice.

Like Mathews, Frank Robinson played the game very hard also. He was on first when somebody hit a line drive base hit toward Hank Aaron in right field. Aaron came up throwing, and Robinson came around second base sort of flying, because he could run real well. He made a hard slide into third base and Aaron's throw was right on the money, one bounce. Eddie, playing the game the way he did, came down with a very hard tag, probably on Frank's head and Frank was out.

Umps sort out a bench-clearing melee at third base between riled up Braves and Reds. An incident of fisticuffs between Ed Mathews and Frank Robinson occurred in that vicinity and this shot could well record the resultant scrum.

Robinson took exception to the tag and came out of the slide with his fists up in a boxing position. Mathews, who always said you hit first and talk later, just hit him with a right and a left and Robinson went down and they literally had to take him out of the game.

Those days were different. The game was played more liberally with less oversight and more physical things were allowed then. Can you imagine that Mathews was not ejected from the game? He threw a combination of punches. The fact that Frank slid hard, that Eddie made what the ump considered a routine tag, and the fact that Robinson came up in an offensive position sort of justified Eddie doing what he did.

Robinson wasn't ejected either, but we really thought he was knocked out. He had to be helped from the field. Eddie

Ed Mathews would like you to have a cigar.

turned around and started clawing the dirt with his spikes, as if to say, OK, that's an out, next batter.

As a tribute to Frank, he actually returned to play the second game with treatment under both eyes and proceeded to hit two home runs in the game.

No doubt about it, Eddie lived a pretty hard life, and was a pretty hard liver. He enjoyed staying out and he enjoyed drinking. We were in Pittsburgh on a Saturday night once with Bob Buhl, also a tough drinker, the only difference between them being that Bob could drink all night and you'd never know it. Eddie would have a few drinks and he really couldn't hold his liquor. He would kind of slobber around and he was tough to handle.

I left him and Buhl in some tavern at about four in the morning. I had tried for a long time to take them back to the hotel, reminding them that we had a doubleheader the next day, Sunday, with the home club Pirates, and that they should get some rest.

Buhl told me later, and he wasn't even pitching, that they were out for about another hour. They pretty much went to bed when it was getting light out.

Mid-morning, a few hours before the game, Eddie showed up at the ballpark and he looked like absolute hell. He was waxing between pale and green at the gills, and we were worried about him.

But there was no need to be. He proceeded in a doubleheader that day to hit four home runs. That was the last time I worried about Eddie answering the bell. He was an unbelievably competitive guy.

While the game was played fiercely, we also sometimes approached the game from a different direction. When they talk about stealing signs, for instance, Joe Adcock was one of the best hitters around when he knew what was coming.

There was a lot of controversy a few years back over the thought that Bobby Thomson, now a Braves teammate, knew what pitch was coming when he banged his famous home run for the Giants to win the pennant over the Dodgers in 1951. It sure didn't surprise me.

We had a system in Milwaukee in those days, in the old County Stadium. Early on the stadium did not have the familiar green walls that we came to know in the outfield, just a wire fence around the gravel track with the bullpen set in right center field.

Bob Buhl was very good at figuring out the signs from the opposing catcher so we used to have Buhl sit out there in the bullpen. He'd watch and it would take Bob about a half an inning to figure out the catcher's sequence of signs.

He could do it even with the bases empty, but if we got somebody on base in the first inning, he could figure out the signs immediately. Teams always changed the signs when there were men on base. My friend Don McMahon would sit right next to Buhl in the bullpen and as soon as McMahon took his hat off, that meant that Buhl had the signs.

There I was warming the bench early in the season, literally not playing because Adcock was such a good hitter when he knew what was coming. This went on for days, weeks at a time, game after game when Joe was healthy. It was working so well that they decided to expand on this thing.

We were going to use it in Wrigley Field. In those days, Wrigley Field didn't sell out or have these huge crowds in the bleachers like today, and most of the time there were very few people sitting out there.

This one typical day in Chicago was sunny and nice. Richie Ashburn was playing center field for them, and Adcock came up, and instead of Buhl and McMahon, this time Buhl and Joey Jay are sitting out in the centerfield bleachers wearing street clothes. McMahon was a relief pitcher and we might need to use him in this particular ball game.

Whoever was pitching to Adcock for the Cubs had to know that Joe had a very tough time hitting hard breaking balls away, but this one particular day, the pitcher threw him a pretty good breaking ball low and away and Joe hit it sharply to right center field.

I mean, he was just right on it so much that Ashburn, playing center field, must have muttered to himself something like, "This just isn't right."

He proceeded to turn and look up into the center field bleachers, only to see two of our ball players sitting up there in street clothes. I'm sure they looked quite dapper, if a bit sheepish.

Within minutes the security people were closing in on Jay and Buhl in right center field and escorted them out. They had caught us cold turkey stealing the signs. At the time, the team got fined and we had to abandon the idea. Perhaps we tried to be a bit more discrete about the practice of stealing signs after that, because habits like that die hard, and they worked.

Late in that glorious season, there was the matter of the afternoon that has kept my name in the record books for more than 50 years. On September 2, in the first game of a double-header in Chicago, I scored six runs in one game.

Adcock was back from his broken leg, and with the short porches in Wrigley Field, I really didn't expect to play that day. Being a bachelor and having a lady friend in Chicago, we spent the evening out and about and the evening went into the morning and I really didn't get to sleep. I went back to the Edgewater Beach Hotel, which is where we were staying, with just enough time to change clothes, take a shower, dress, go to church and get to the ball park with zero sleep.

I arrived at Clark and Sheffield a bit groggy and ambled into the clubhouse, only to look into the trainer's room and see Adcock spread out on the training table with a bad back. Consequently, I found myself playing a doubleheader in the 95-degree heat with no sleep and more than a little fuzzy-headed from the night before. I'm sure I made Ernie Banks proud that day by playing two.

In the first game, I got on base seven times. I had three or four hits (Frank had four—two singles and two doubles)[9], the rest walks, maybe a sacrifice or two, and tied a Major League record, scoring six runs in a game. It was like being on a merry-go-round. I was on third base for the seventh time with the Braves ahead about 23 to ten when Eddie Mathews made the

The magnificent Ernie Banks of the Chicago Cubs, as slender and supple a slugger as ever slung lumber. Banks was twice named National League Most Valuable Player.

last out in the top of the ninth on a shallow fly ball to the outfield.

I could conceivably have set the record in a nine-inning game. I should have tried to steal home. I'm still one of several people tied with six runs scored in a game, including Mel Ott, who did it twice, and a few guys from the 1890s.

When somebody with the Mets (Edgardo Alfonso) later scored that many runs in a game, the world was shocked to see my name among the others with the tie. The second game that day went only about five innings, of course, because Wrigley Field in those days had no lights. The game was suspended because of darkness.

After we showered, my roommate, Johnny Logan and I went over to the Gaslight Club at the Palmer House to have dinner and celebrate and I ordered a drink. I was more than a little tired and before my drink arrived, my head was down on

All eyes are on the field, as speedster and power-hitting center fielder Richie Ashburn waits on deck for the Philadelphia Phillies. Ashburn was a lifetime .308 hitter in 15 campaigns.

the table and I was asleep. Knowing Johnny, he ate and drank right around me.

But with the kind of year we were having, things just kind of fell into place. Even though we sustained some key injuries, notably to Covington and Bruton in the outfield, others picked up the slack. A kid we brought up from the minor leagues became one of those legends, and he became known as Bob "Hurricane" Hazle.

The Braves had a very good farm system at the time and we had two or three potential call-ups when we needed an outfielder that 1957 season. One of our better scouts of the time told our management people that even though this guy wasn't on their list, that at that moment down in AAA ball, Bob Hazle was hitting the ball better than anyone. He was really on a streak and the scout recommended very strongly that we bring him up instead of two or three other guys that this scout was really down there to look at.

Hazle was just killing opposing pitching and they brought him in late July. I remember when it was first announced that a guy named Bob Hazle was coming up to the big leagues,

Frank Torre, ever fleet afoot, charges to the plate against Philadelphia, his spikes barely touching the ground.

A sartorially splendid Frank Torre likely with the equally dapper Humberto Robinson, a Braves pitcher from 1955-1958, *Chicago Sun-Times* in hand.

Joey Jay, hard-throwing Milwaukee Braves right hander, and keen interpreter of opposing team's signs, bears down before the Wrigley ivy. Jay had consecutive 21 win seasons in 1961 and 1962.

we all sort of looked at each other and said, "Who is he, where is he coming from?" Actually the Braves had obtained him in the trade for George Crowe early the year before. He arrived from our AAA club in Wichita.

When I tell you about this individual, the rest is basically history, because he hit everybody, and anybody, lefties, righties. He was a slightly built, left-hand hitter, and I mean he hit everybody hard.

If there is such a thing as hitting a hard .400, he hit a hard .400 because he didn't get any cheap hits. Without him, we would have never accomplished what we did. In something like 40 games he hit .403, knocked in about 30 runs and banged seven out of the park.

He didn't have a particularly good World Series, with just a couple of hits, but August and September that year belonged to Bob Hazle. The writers started calling him "Hurricane" after about a week.

Over August 9 and 10th, Hazle goes seven for ten and drives in five runs in two big wins over the Cardinals. August 15th, he gets another three hits including a homer as we beat Cincinnati. August 25th, the Hurricane delivers two three-run home runs and since coming up from Wichita is hitting .526.

In the game where I scored six times, Hazle had four hits. In the very thick of the pennant race late in September, after the Braves had lost eight of 11 games, and we were stumbling, raising the specter of the swoon of '56, we finally won in Chicago on a tenth-inning homer by Hazle. It was his 21st run batted in since his first for us on July 31. We clinched the pennant the next day.

The tragic part of the whole situation for Bob was that over the winter, they pretty much wrote him off. The Braves really didn't give him a chance the next year and he got shipped over to Detroit.

Bob "Hurricane" Hazle, whose clutch hitting (.403 with 27 RBIs) in late summer of 1957 played a major role in bringing the National League pennant to Milwaukee.

SUMMER OF THE HURRICANE

If you were a kid between the ages of 5 and 75 pulling for the Milwaukee Braves in the summer of 1957, you had to groan and grimace with the season-ending knee injury of star center fielder Billy Bruton. Bruton had hit the very first home run in the brand new Milwaukee County Stadium four years earlier, was the mainstay for the club in center field, a real speedster on the base paths and a lightning streak out in center, ranging the green expanse between the rising star Henry Aaron out in right and the powerful slugger Wes Covington over in left, who also was hurt earlier that season.

When Bruton went down, it was a shock to the Braves' pennant hopes, especially after their 1956 "September Swoon" where the club faded and lost the lead to the Brooklyn Dodgers in the final days of the season.

Hoping to pick up Bruton's slack, the Braves dug down into their minor league system, locating a certain Robert Sydney Hazle with their Wichita, Kansas club, where he'd come over in a trade for Milwaukee Braves original George Crowe earlier in the year.

Hazle was no green rookie but a 26-year old minor league roustabout who was hitting a decent .279 with the triple A club, and who'd led the Southern Association with 29 home runs two years earlier in 1955.

So now he gets the call to join the big league club 100 games into the season, entering a stellar Braves locker room loaded with the likes of Ed Mathews, Henry Aaron, Red Schoendienst, Johnny Logan, Warren Spahn, and Lew Burdette.

Unfazed and batting left-handed, Hazle unpacked a fearsome piece of lumber that might as well have had a lightning streak emblazoned on it, because he proceeded to tear up the league, and many say, make the Milwaukee pennant dream possible that hot, legendary summer.

Sliding nicely into the line-up, and playing right field sometimes with Aaron moving deftly into center, and sometimes center, Hazle began to pound out hits at a torrid pace. They talk about his legendary month, from late July to the end of August with 34 hits in 67 at bats, hitting .507, scoring 16 runs and knocking in 21 more.

He literally tore it up, and somewhere about a week or two into this historic offensive outburst, he was dubbed "Hurricane" in the press, and Hurricane Hazle for the ages he became.

If August was torrid for the Hurricane, September was merely rambunctious, since after the league had seen his first swings around the circuit they slowed him down to a more worldly 20 for 63 and a .317 average the rest of the way.

For his two months in the regular line-up that summer, Bob "Hurricane" Hazle had posted a .403 batting average, and games in which he was a deciding factor were many.

On August 25 against the Phillies he nailed two three-run home runs, with a single and a walk for good measure. On September 22, he pounded out three doubles, singled, and drove in two runs as the Braves buried the Cubs 23-10 in a then-record setting avalanche of runs and hits with 26. In the other game of the September 22 double-header, he hit a 10th inning ball out of the park that stood up for win. On September 6 he homered in a 5-4 win over the Cubs.

A model of base-hit consistency, he went 4-5 in a 13-2 win against St. Louis, August 9. He was 3 for 4 in a 9-0 win the next day. He went 3 for 4 in consecutive wins against Cincinnati in the middle of August, and 3 for 4 later in the month in a win over Brooklyn.

Only once in that month did he go down swinging, 0 for 4 against St. Louis August 17 in a 5-0 Braves victory.

Hazle's bat lit the way and his nickname glamorized the headlines and become synonymous with Milwaukee's surging run at the pennant.

As the Braves caught fire, passed the St. Louis Cardinals to take the lead in the National League standings, and then put some distance between the two clubs heading into the World Series, the Hurricane came ashore, and was downgraded from a CAT 5 to a CAT 3 to a tropical storm.

He saw little action in the seven-game Braves World Series win over the Yankees, hitting .154, but did get his two hits in game seven, scoring the first run in the Braves 5-0 triumph over the Bronx Bombers. Hazle then got little playing time for the Braves in 1958, and found himself traded to the Detroit Tigers, where within that year his major league career played itself out.

A Hurricane, sure, but also a comet, a meteorite of spectacular hitting that turned the National League on its ear at a time when the Milwaukee Braves needed it most. Bob "Hurricane" Hazle pounded his name indelibly into the baseball history books. It's highly likely the Braves would not have won that 1957 pennant without him, as he put the minds and hearts of Braves fans from 5 to 75 at ease that legendary, distant summer.

We never really expected Hazle to play as a regular. He was going to hit against right-handers, but with all our injuries in the outfield, he had opportunities to play and hit and he took the world by storm. He was a super-nice guy, a true gentleman from South Carolina.

Early on in the 1957 season, though, things were not all peaches and cream and we were not playing all that well. We were in about second or third place and I don't recall exactly how it happened, but Adcock broke his leg.

There were a lot of comments made by a lot of people then, that the Braves were finished because now without Adcock, we had no chance. And quite frankly, because of the suddenness of the accident, the club didn't have time to react, so I had to play, and I really performed well. I wasn't flashy or anything else, but I made all the plays in the field. My mantra about needing to play regularly bore fruit for me because it was true. I got an awful lot of clutch hits. At some point, I cracked a bone in a finger. I had been hitting even higher than the .272 that I finished with, but just like with a damaged knee in my rookie

Frank Torre and Nippy Jones, classic peers at the first-base position.

FRANK THE DEFENDER

Frank Torre demonstrates winning first-base form. He had a lifetime .993 fielding percentage with only 28 errors versus 3,872 chances and 3,536 put-outs.

Frank Torre in a cloud of dust works a close pick-off play at first base against the Cubs.

Frank records the put-out of a Pirate at first base in the summer sun.

Frank Torre secures ball in glove and puts a tag on a Cubs batter with an eye on the plate while holding runners at first and third

Frank applies the tag from an errant throw to a streaking Red.

year, this was not a time to back off. You play through it when there is no tomorrow.

They did go out and get Nippy Jones later and he played against some left-handers. But for the most part, I played consistently, hit well, fielded my position as always, and we won the pennant.

Right at the end of the season, Adcock was getting healthy. Even though I had been the first baseman through most of the year, he came back and started the World Series at first base.

I played in every World Series game, and only batted ten times. I started three of the games in the Series though, including game seven, and I always came in for him late in the game for defensive purposes.

That season, it was great playing every day and contributing. I had to know my role because once we got Schoendienst, he took another bunch of points off my average. He was leading

In full stride, Ed Mathews launches what looks to be merely a high fly ball.

Red Schoendienst occupies a practice on-deck circle. Schoendienst averaged 179 hits and 31 doubles a year over 19 major league seasons.

off and I was hitting second. He led off an awful lot of games with doubles and my assignment was to get him over to third. That's all part of the team concept to winning ball games. It's sort of a lost art today, sacrificing the man over to third.

Red at one time was considered fast, but when we had him he was more quick than fast. He didn't bunt his way on base much. He was a switch-hitter and a very tough out.

Often Mathews and Aaron flip-flopped batting third and fourth. Schoendienst led off, I hit second. Mathews and Aaron would switch, depending on who was pitching for the other team, because left-handers didn't bother Eddie. Usually he hit third and Hank hit fourth.

When Schoendienst led off games with doubles, probably ten or twelve times during the season, I would go 0-for-one just hitting a ground ball to the second base side to move our first runner over to third. It was just a matter of who was up next as to who always knocked in the run.

Billy Muffett teed up the pitch that Henry Aaron planted over the center field fence to clinch the National League pennant for the Milwaukee Braves in 1957.

Now the City of Milwaukee late that summer was a bit concerned about us going down the stretch because of our September swoon in 1956, and you couldn't blame the fans. But in 1957 we took the pennant by eight games over the Cardinals. I wouldn't say we coasted. Our lead dwindled to about four or five games as we started to take a little bit of a nose dive in the final weeks before we seemed to get a shot of adrenaline and picked back up.

We won rather easily then, but only after the unforgettable night late in September when Henry Aaron stepped up to the plate in the bottom of the 11th against the St. Louis Cardinals, who were technically still in the race.

I had a bit part earlier in the 10th, grounding into a double play with the bases jammed full of Braves. This was another

Henry Aaron is mobbed by exultant teammates crossing the plate after the home run that clinched the National League pennant for the Milwaukee Braves in 1957. A Milwaukee County Stadium usher tries to keep Aaron upright with a palm under his chin. Warren Spahn is at Aaron's right elbow, and Frank Torre jogging at his left, as Wes Covington and Felix Mantilla appear to hold the home run hero up by his waist and legs. Characteristically, Ed Mathews takes the great moment in stride at the back of the pack.

instance where my speed afoot came into play. Bud Selig always kidded me about my running time down to first base. "I could run faster backward than Frank could forward," I think Bud said at the time. It was probably true, although later he was being chased around by club owners and members of Congress.

In the 11th inning, Logan singled himself on board. With two outs, and by some accounts it was 11:34 p.m., Henry jumped all over the first pitch from Billy Muffett and pounded it out to center field. For a second it appeared that Wally Moon had pulled in the drive with a leaping grab, but a mad scramble of fans for the ball on the other side of the fence made it clear—the Braves had won the pennant. We were going to the World Series. Henry was carried off the field. Bedlam broke loose all around town. I'm told parents woke their sleeping children with the news: *"The Braves won!"*

THE 1957 WORLD SERIES

GAME ONE

The Yankees took game one in New York 2-1. Whitey Ford was the winner and Spahnnie took the loss. I started out on the bench and went in late in the game, as I called it, for a cup of coffee. What I most recall is what an awesome thing it was coming out for the World Series in New York at Yankee Stadium with all the media on the field and the fans in the stands.

Attendance that night was 69,000 plus and it was not like today where they control the crowd on the field before a game. I don't suppose just anybody could walk out there, but security was loose.

Fred Haney, Milwaukee Braves manager, leans in for shop talk with Yankees Manager Casey Stengel, in a dugout close-up. The two managers split against each other in two World Series, each winning a Series in seven games, Haney for the Braves in 1957, Stengel for the damn Yankees in 1958. Stengel alienated Milwaukee fans during the '57 series, allegedly calling Milwaukee a "bush" town.[10]

Before the game, you couldn't even play catch because there were so many people on the field, milling around, conducting interviews, cajoling, patting us on the back, getting autographs.

Even though I was from New York and we were the Braves, a strong club with our own stars, the fact that you see the Yankees out there and the Yankees were like, Jesus Christ Superstar, just gives you pause. I attribute us losing the first game basically to our being in awe and a bit tight. It took us the first game to really loosen up and play baseball. We were kind of hypnotized by the fact that we were in the World Series.

Seeing my brother's success later with the Yankees, I think one of the advantages the Yankees have playing year in and year out is the fact that they've been there so many times. Most of their players have been in the World Series and every other club has to overcome that when they play the Yankees.

Of course, the biggest obstacle of all was dealing with tickets. Most people don't realize it was difficult even in those days to get World Series tickets; players had to pay for them as well.

Essentially, a player is paying for tickets and giving them away. I had a very difficult time with some of my relatives. Naturally, for my mother, my sister, and my brothers, they were on me. No way was my sister the cloistered nun going to attend, but I expected to get paid by some of my uncles. Actually, they were a lot better off financially than I was. One uncle was a liquor salesman and he insisted on paying me with booze. Just what I needed.

I stayed at the hotel with the team, at a place called the Commodore Hotel, now a Hyatt. We were bused to Yankee Stadium all together. Had I stayed at home in Brooklyn, I would have had to drive a lot further to Yankee Stadium, and

The Glory Years

Masterful New York Yankees left-hander Whitey Ford, who Frank Torre said, "would give you ice in the wintertime."

the chaos of being at home in the neighborhood while trying to concentrate on the World Series would have been too much.

Not taking anything away from Whitey Ford in the first game, because he was a hell of a pitcher, and an even greater money pitcher, but so was Spahn, and we had some pretty good hitters. It almost appeared like we were going through the motions in game one. I don't think we relaxed until late in the game. We only scraped up a single run on five hits and went down in sort of a daze.

Covington went 2-4 and scored the Braves' one run, as Aaron, Mathews, Logan and Adcock were a combined 1-14, with Aaron playing center field and getting a hit and Mathews walking twice. Andy Pafko played right field and went hitless in four at-bats. Frank Torre did not bat and appeared for defensive purposes late as the Braves left seven men stranded. Taking the loss, Spahn lasted only five and one-third innings, and gave up all three runs on seven hits. He was spelled by Ernie Johnson and Don McMahon in relief. Whitey Ford for the Yankees took the win, scattering five Braves' hits and walking four.

GAME TWO

Game two we win 4-2. Burdette gets his first win, Johnny Logan hits a home run. We broke a 2-2 tie in the fourth on three singles, and an error by Tony Kubek, a nice Milwaukee, Wisconsin boy. Covington makes his first spectacular catch to kill a Yankees threat in the second.

Throughout the Series, Burdette was a surprise hero to all of us. Ultimately, he was the lead story of this World Series with his three magnificent victories, including the final 5-0 shutout in game seven for our fourth win. He was one of our steady pitchers, but nobody ever dreamed that he would be such a great pitcher in the World Series against the Yankees. Again, I entered the game, but late.

Leaping Wes Covington, Milwaukee Braves slugger and left-fielder, distinguished himself with his glove in the field with great catches in the 1957 World Series.

Naturally, getting a split at Yankee Stadium was a big deal for us, because by now we felt pretty confident that we had as good a team as anybody in the world. We had a feeling that we were going to win the World Series, but it still was a big relief to take that second game. You don't like to fall behind to anybody two games to zip, especially not New York.

After getting that split, we were feeling pretty good, going back to Milwaukee tied one and one for game three. We liked playing on our home grounds and in front of our wonderful fans.

On the travel day, Casey Stengel, the Yankees manager, threw more wood on the fire when he came out in the newspapers calling Milwaukee a hick town. I think he said we were "bush league." Without any additional incentives, Milwaukee had been all souped up and excited, but with Casey making that statement, it really put everyone in an uproar.

The folks in town were already really behind us. We had set an all-time major league attendance record at the time, and they were boisterous and loud in the stands, but Casey's comments seemed to change their personality and make them even louder and more intense. We could see it, and feel it.

The Braves made their eight hits count, scoring four times including on Logan's home run and a triple by Aaron. Covington again went 2-4 as did Adcock with each driving in a run. Frank Torre again wielded his glove late in the game without batting. Despite a Hank Bauer home run and an Enos Slaughter double, Burdette pitched all nine innings and dispersed seven Yankee hits for the win. Bobby Shantz took the loss giving up six hits and all four Braves runs in just three innings, as relievers Ditmar and Grim followed to two-hit the Braves over the final six innings.

GAME THREE

With one day off between contests, we came home to Milwaukee for game three. Bob Turley opens against Bob Buhl, and Don Larsen gets the win. Buhl, Pizarro, Conley, Johnson, Trowbridge, and McMahon all pitch for the Braves and we go down 12-3, handing them 11 walks. The big story, other than that we got clobbered, was hometown boy Tony Kubek belting two home runs.

Our starting pitcher, Buhl, just never found himself. Bob couldn't get anybody out and neither could most of the gang that followed him to the mound. Once you open the flood gates like that, it's Katie bar the door.

I finally got a chance to hit, getting in a bit earlier in this World Series game, and I grounded out in the one at-bat I had. Nothing you can say about the loss though. The pitching was not there and the Yanks handed us our heads.

Don Larsen, the heroic Yankees pitcher, whose perfect game against the Dodgers in the 1956 World Series will always shine. Larsen was big trouble for the Braves in the 1958 World Series, although the Braves for the most part escaped his wizardry in 1957, excepting his game three win.

Frank was 0-2 in his two trips to the plate. Braves bats woke up a bit in the loss with Schoendienst going 3-5, Logan 2-4 and Aaron 2-5, with one of his being a home run shot off of Larsen in the fifth. But the Braves also wasted seven men who reached base on walks leaving a total of 14 runners stranded. One of Kubek's home-runs was off Buhl and one off Trowbridge. Mickey Mantle homered off of Conley in the fourth. Buhl took the loss although he picked Mickey Mantle off of second base. Only Ernie Johnson pitched scoreless innings (2) for the Milwaukee club. Yankees starting pitcher Bob Turley lasted only an inning and two-thirds, as Larsen threw seven and a third in relief. They each walked four. Ed Mathews drew three walks in the contest.

GAME FOUR

Little did I know, however, that what had transpired in game three was a break for me, Frank Torre. After that trouncing, Fred Haney made up his mind that he was going to make a few changes. I was afforded the opportunity to start game four.

Adcock had not really been hitting well since he came back in the middle of September.

Adcock was 2-11 in the series to this point, but Mathews was 0-8, although he had walked five times.

In Joe Adcock's defense, he was still coming off the broken leg. He just hadn't been tearing down the fences like everyone expected and I was glad for the start.

Tom Sturdivant started against us in this pivotal game. We were down two games to one and they went through Shantz, Kucks, Byrne and Grim trying to keep it close.

We came up with four runs in the fourth inning. Three of our four runs came when Hank hit a home run with a man on and a solo shot I hit out of the park.

Bobby Shantz, three-time All Star and veteran hurler won 24 games in 1952. The Braves kept him and other Yankee pitchers largely at bay in the 1957 World Series.

Frank Torre connects with a powerful swing from his lefty side of the plate. Frank hit five triples in each of the 1957 and 1958 seasons. His two home runs in the 1957 World Series contributed to the Braves' championship crown.

My home run went to right center field. Even though I hit five home runs that year, that was my first ever in Milwaukee, and what a time for it. Not that I was much of a home run hitter period. But it was quite a thrill to say the least. I hardly even remember running around the bases. Sturdivant gave me a fastball sort of over the inside part of the plate and I knew I hit it well, but not being used to hitting the ball over the fence, I never dreamed it was going to be a home run.

When I got between first and second and then you get the sign from the umpire that it was over the fence, then you know. But it was hard to tell the difference because with the wire fence you sometimes couldn't tell if it was over or not. It was more of a line drive. But once the umpire gave the wave, I could slow down. I wonder if Bud Selig could tell when I went into my trot.

In those days, County Stadium wasn't an easy park to hit home runs in. Later they put a different fence out there and enclosed the field quite a bit and the ball carried much better.

When I was with Aaron and Mathews, we used to wonder how many more home runs they would have hit if the same conditions had existed in the early years when they played. It really was a pitcher's ballpark—whether it was a bad carry or the winds coming in from the Veterans' Home on the hill or the chocolate breezes wafting in from Johnston's Cookie factory across the highway.

We jumped to a 4-to-1 lead and Spahnnie, who went the distance through ten innings, took the lead into the ninth. But with two outs, he gave up singles to Berra and McDougald. On a 3-to-2 count, Elston Howard homered to left and tied the game. Who would have thought Spahnnie could blow the lead?

We did nothing in our half of the inning, and in the 10th, Kubek got on and Hank Bauer tripled him in. Warren Spahn was still on the mound in the 10th after giving up a go-ahead

Warren Spahn goes into his wind-up.

triple, but he bore down and retired the side. It could never happen today, where the starter, after giving up the lead twice, stays in the game, even in extra innings.

We were down 5-to-4 in the 10th when Nippy Jones came up to bat, pinch-hitting for Spahn. Our fate hung by a shoelace. Here is this journeyman first baseman, who until we picked him up from the Pacific Coast League, hadn't played in the majors in five years.

With nobody out and nobody on, the first pitch goes low and inside, hits Nippy on the shoe, and skips off into the dirt. Nippy started to take his base, but the umpire, Augie Donatelli, called it a ball. Nippy said the ball had hit his foot.

Now there are conflicting accounts of what happened. By one account, the ball boy or a Milwaukee trainer came up and presented Donatelli with the ball showing a black scuff mark from Nippy's freshly polished shoe. Nippy says he and Yogi each made a lunge for the ball and Nippy came up with it and

Nippy Jones' newly polished shoes gave the Braves a chance to win game four of the 1957 World Series. Jones had been out of baseball for five years when the Braves brought him up behind Frank Torre after Joe Adcock went down with a broken leg earlier in the season. Jones was a lifetime .267 hitter over eight seasons, posting a .300 batting average with the Cardinals in 1949 in 380 at-bats. Like Frank, he produced when given the chance. In 1948, he recorded a career high 81 RBIs. His final career at-bat and the famous shoe-polish incident turned the '57 series back to the Braves.

presented it to Donatelli, who, when he saw the evidence, immediately awarded Nippy first base.

Tommy Ferguson, who was our clubhouse guy and did all the polishing of the shoes, later got a special commendation from the club. My recollection is that when the umpire initially didn't give Nippy first base, one of our coaches insisted on checking the ball, and there was a big black spot of shoe polish on it.

There was a bit of an argument from the Yankees, but it was pretty much cut and dried. We all stayed on the bench. Nippy took his base, and that was the key to the inning. Who knows what might have happened if Nippy hadn't gotten on.

Fortunately Nippy had just gone into the game. If he'd been in the game for a few innings, maybe the polish would have worn down a little bit, but Nippy's fresh shoeshine made the black mark stand out on the ball and there was no doubt about it because it became a well photographed baseball.

After the game and for the next few days, it was a much-talked-about play, but I don't think anybody complained about the decision made. The evidence was clear.

As to the ironies of baseball, for Nippy, Milwaukee was his last stop. That play, which will forever survive in the history books, was also his last trip to the plate in the major leagues.

Felix Mantilla substituted for Nippy as the base runner. The stage was set. Johnny Logan came up and Haney gave the third base coach the bunt sign for Logan to get the tying run to second. Whether he missed the sign or ignored it, Logan didn't bunt. John was a clutch hitter and it's not to say you're supposed to ignore signs when somebody gives them to you because certain people are paid to manage and others are paid to play, but he did ignore it. He hit a double off Bob Grim and got the tying run across the plate as Felix Mantilla scored.

The fiercely competitive Milwaukee Braves shortstop, four-time All-Star Johnny Logan, arrived with the team from Boston.

Ever-ready player Felix Mantilla at times held down virtually every position on the field other than pitcher and catcher, recording a lifetime fielding percentage of .966 in 11 seasons. Felix was a National League All-Star in 1965. Felix scored the tying run in the tenth inning of game four of the 1957 World Series.

That brought up Mathews. Eddie had not had a hit in the three previous games and came up now with only a single in game four. He was one for 11 in the Series and way overdue. With Logan taking a lead off second, Eddie caught one in his wheelhouse the way only he could and drove it over the right field fence. The place went berserk.

Here we had salvaged a game, 7-to-5, that we had apparently salted away earlier, with Spahn on the mound, only to seemingly fritter it away in both the ninth and tenth innings.

I'll never forget after the game and Mathews' home run that won it. Fred Haney was naturally very happy. If we go down three to one with the Yankees it probably would have been "door closed." Haney went over to congratulate Logan, but Logan was still burning because of Haney wanting him to bunt and John just refused to shake his manager's hand.

After Mathews hit that home run, he took it in stride. He was such a pro. Naturally he was excited, but he wasn't a real emotional guy. I'm sure that he felt as great as everybody else, except he kept it pretty much within himself. It also was gratifying to him after going hitless three games straight.

And how about Spahn? See, that's the difference in the times. In today's game of baseball, a starting pitcher would never survive that long. Number one, it would have been questionable if Spahn even started the ninth inning. Now, you would have had a closer in there. But pitchers then were trained to pitch nine or ten innings barring complete disaster, and that's what they did.

When I hit mine out earlier in the game, the stadium went crazy with the noise, but going around the bases, I don't even remember my feet touching the ground. Brother Joe and my sister were up in the stands. Plus, my mother was wearing a hat and she had been overly generous with the good seats we had and gave them away. So my family was sitting in the upper deck. Mom got so excited that she started to wave the hat and actually threw it out of the stands. Running around the bases, I literally saw this hat fly out of the stands and never realized at the time that it was my mother's. She lost it, of course. I felt pretty good. I felt like I was on top of the world.

The next morning, my mother and I were asked to appear on the *NBC Today* show. Mom had been on the plane from New York to Milwaukee with some of the *Today* folks and they had been giving her champagne and they were quite impressed with her. When she was asked on the air the obligatory question,

"Who's your favorite ballplayer?" without hesitation she replied. "Gil Hodges." Honesty always ran in the family, and Mom always kept us honest.

Elston Howard's three-run home run blast off of Warren Spahn in the ninth was the Yankees decisive play. Hank Bauer also tripled in a run off of Spahn. Logan and Mathews were each 2-4. Aaron and Frank Torre each homered off of Sturdi-vant, as Mathews took Grim deep to right field in the tenth for the walk-off win.

GAME FIVE

Burdette came out and again beat Whitey Ford, 1-to-0. Adcock's single in the sixth drove in the only run after Covington's catch robbed Gil McDougald of a possible home run in the fourth. This was Wes' second amazing catch of the series.

For Joe Adcock, after the tough season he'd had, it was a great hit. He got the start against the left-handed pitcher, Ford. I came in the game late for defense after he got the key hit. That was the game.

Except that Eddie Mathews, and this doesn't show up, was crucial in that game. He hit a regular ground ball to second base. While Jerry Coleman didn't nonchalant it, he just assumed he had Eddie nailed at first. Instead of charging in and hustling it, he just played the ball routinely.

Eddie was deceptively fast running down to first, and hustling all the way, he beat the throw. He actually was the run that scored when Adcock got that two-out, game-winning hit.

Who knows how many innings we might have played had not Eddie beat it out. Whitey wasn't exactly easy to score on and if you were going to beat him, you had to get the kind of pitching we had in that game.

And of course, Burdette did his magic again. He pitched an outstanding ball game. It was naturally a very critical game because we knew we had to go back to Yankee Stadium. Going back there up three games to two was a hell of a lot better than going to have to win two in a row.

Although Hank Bauer was 2-4 and Enos Slaughter 2-3, the powerful Yankees line-up came up scoreless before Lew Burdette's seven-hit, five-strike-out performance. Burdette was now 2-0 in the Series. The Braves rang up three double plays in the game. Aaron went 2-3, as did Pafko, but Adcock's two-out RBI scoring Mathews proved the difference. Ford threw seven innings to record the loss.

GAME SIX

In game six, Bob Buhl opened against Turley, who went nine innings for New York. Again, Aaron and I hit home runs in the game.

I felt really good at the plate. I was in a good groove where I was seeing the ball really well, and the one time Turley got me out, I hit a line drive back to the pitcher. My home run was again a line drive where the bullpen used to be in Yankee Stadium.

We were behind 3-2 and I was on deck in the ninth inning when Covington came up with a man on first and one out. Strange as it might seem, I felt very good about coming up with an opportunity to maybe win the game because I was seeing the ball from Turley really well. I was a good fast-ball hitter and he was a fast-ball pitcher.

I was hoping beyond hope that I'd get the opportunity. Unfortunately, Wes hit the ball sharply right back to the mound, they got a double play, and that was the end of the game.

As to my home run, well, it was a very tight game. I came up with nobody on base and I was playing in my hometown at Yankee Stadium.

By no means was I a Yankees fan, because I hated the Yankees, and the hit was potentially very big for the team. I was a Giants fan because my father was a Giants fan and we grew up that way, even though we lived in Brooklyn.

In this instance, I got a good pitch to hit and I hit it hard. Again, I didn't think it was high enough to go out, but it carried. Other than the fact that we weren't ahead in the ball game, it was a hell of a feeling, hitting a home run in your hometown in the World Series in front of family and friends.

What took away from the thrill is the fact that we didn't win the game. I would have given the home run back if we could have won the game and gotten it over with. That was October 9th.

Frank Torre was the only Brave with two hits in the game, including his home run, in three at-bats. Aaron's hit was a home run also off Turley. After Buhl gave up two Yankee runs, Braves reliever Ernie Johnson took the loss while giving up only two hits and striking out five in four and a third innings, as Hank Bauer took him deep to left with the bases empty in the seventh. Braves pitchers combined to fan nine Yanks. Eight Braves went down swinging.

GAME SEVEN

I was lucky enough to draw the start in the seventh game of the World Series against the Yankees in '57.

Spahn came down with a flu bug and Burdette pitched on two days' rest. We were going up against Don Larsen. Here's the guy who had pitched a perfect game in the World Series the year before, opening against us in game seven on his field, and Mr. Burdette shuts them out.

Del Crandall hit a home run. A Kubek error paved the way for four runs in the third. Tony had a few problems with errors in the series.

Tony was a good ball player and a really good fielder, and everybody has those kind of streaks. For him, it had its bitter and its sweet because he was playing against his hometown. I guess he wanted to do good so bad, and he'd had a great game against us when they kicked our butts earlier and he hit those two home runs. But the way that Burdette pitched, Tony Kubek didn't lose that ball game. Burdette was in such a groove that he could have pitched all day.

I was lucky to get an RBI in the game. Bobby Shantz had come in to pitch, and I came up with men on first and third. I was pretty much looking over my shoulder. I thought for sure that Fred was going to pinch hit with Adcock or some right

The irrepressible right-hander Lew Burdette notched three wins over the New York Yankees and was World Series Most Valuable Player in 1957. In the 1958 Series, he lost two games including game seven on two day's rest, and picked up one win, for a 4-2 career post-season record. His 1957 World Series ERA was 0.67.

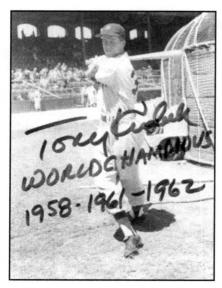

World Champion Milwaukeean Tony Kubek was not conflicted in the slightest battling against his hometown Braves and anchoring infield positions for the New York Yankees. In his own hand, he was a World Series Champion in 1958, 1961, and 1962.

hand hitter to get another run across. To my surprise, and I guess that's one of the reasons I wasn't as alert as I normally was, I missed a squeeze bunt sign.

Fortunately, I hit a ground ball to second base and as slow-footed as I normally am, I must have realized that I had to do something special. I seemed to come up with a little extra juice and beat the throw to first. We scored the run. Even though Fred Haney wasn't too happy that I missed the sign, it didn't cost us anything.

After the game and we'd won the World Series, he came over to me in the locker and said I was lucky that I had got that hit.

Even with Burdette cruising along pretty easily during most of the game, in the ninth inning, as good teams like the Yankees usually do, they started to come back. They had two outs but we couldn't retire the third batter and they wound up loading the bases.

Moose Skowron, a strong right-handed hitter came up and got good wood on the ball. He hit it really pretty hard right over the bag at third, and Eddie, by now a first-class fielder, made an outstanding back-handed stop on a short hop. His momentum carried him forward and he just stepped on third base and the game and the Series were history.

The only thing disappointing as a team was that we didn't win it in Milwaukee. For me it was thrilling because we did it in my own back yard. But because of the importance of celebrating with our Milwaukee fans, we had to tone ourselves down and get to Milwaukee in a sober state of mind and body. We would do our celebrating when we got back—which our fans helped us do in abundance.

Naturally, we all piled together on the field, me running over from first base. I had played all nine innings of game seven.

Bill "Moose" Skowron had a great regular season in 1957, but was not much of a factor in the World Series that year. Wait 'til next year may never have had such import, however.

We splashed some champagne over ourselves for the cameras and flew back to Milwaukee late that afternoon. It was a day game, which most Series' games were then.

Upon our arrival, we took a heck of a drive to a bash of some sort. The fans were wild, there was ticker tape, and not planned ticker tape either. It was spontaneous. The hometowners were literally emptying their offices and desks out onto the street as we passed by.

The people of Milwaukee were out there cheering and screaming and grabbing and the whole town was celebrating and we celebrated pretty much most of the night.

Milwaukeeans pour into the streets to celebrate as the Milwaukee Braves beat the New York Yankees in seven games to win the 1957 baseball World Series— just days after Yankees manager Casey Stengel called Milwaukee a "bush" town.

In typical Frank Torre fashion, at six o'clock in the morning, I was swimming in Lake Michigan. You sober up pretty quickly at dawn in the frigid waves of a Great Lake in October.

I lived on Prospect Avenue near the beach and we carried the party over in that direction, feeling no pain, a whole bunch of us. I'm not sure exactly which of the ball players were there, Del Rice was one of them for sure in the group at the time, and it was a "let's go for a swim" type of thing.

Well, you don't dare do this in October in Lake Michigan. I'm told you don't do it there in July, but one dared the other and then a whole bunch of us—including me—took the plunge.

The next day we sat back and took a deep breath. We just enjoyed being the world champs. I think it sank in during the

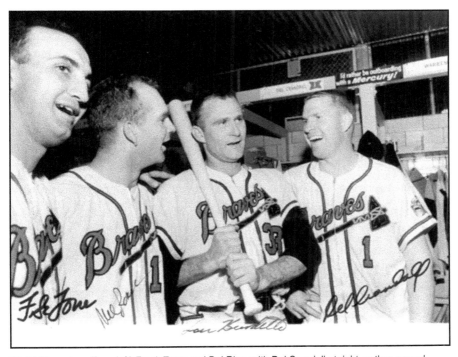

World Champions (from left) Frank Torre and Del Rice, with Del Crandall at right, gather around fine-hitting pitcher Lew Burdette.

plane ride back from New York to Milwaukee, maybe sipping a glass of champagne. You realize that you're one of 25 players on the best team in the world, and that's quite a statement to make. Being young, just 26, I didn't realize the importance of the achievement until much later, when it dawned on me how tough it was to do that.

It had been a dramatic Series, but without great pitching from Burdette, it might not have been. The team did not exactly knock the cover off the ball. I hit .300 for the series, Aaron hit .393, Red hit .278, but Mathews hit .227, Covington .208, Logan .185, Adcock .200, Pafko .214, and Bob Hazle only hit .154. We were kind of a mixed bag at the plate.

Other than that one game when the Yankees kicked our brains in, the games were won with pitching, clutch-hitting, and defense.

Covington probably deserved as much credit as anyone, even though he didn't hit his weight. He made some great plays in Yankee Stadium and going into the Series, there had been comments like, "Watch what a circus it's going to be when Wes Covington goes to the difficult left field in Yankee Stadium. He'll make a fool of himself."

Wes was not respected as a fielder up until that time. But what does he do? He turns around and makes two or three sensational catches out there that saved at least one game and perhaps two. The team overall played really good defense and Wes was sterling in the field.

You've got to give the Yankee pitching some credit. Whitey Ford will give you ice in the wintertime. Turley, Sturdivant, and Don Larsen, weren't exactly chopped steak. Ford's ERA was 1.13, Turley's was 2.31, but it's pretty hard to beat Burdette's 0.67. And over 27 innings. He was unbelievable. He only walked four people.

Hazle showed up in this game and went 2-4, scoring once. Mathews went 1-4 with two RBIs and scored once. Frank Torre got an RBI and walked twice. Logan scored once going one for five. Aaron scored once with two hits in five at-bats. Seven Yankees hits produced zero runs as they left nine stranded. Recording a third 1957 World Series win, Burdette gave up seven hits and walked one en route to being named Series MVP. Don Larsen was handed the Yankees loss with only two and one third innings pitched.

In 1957, the winning share for each player was $8,900, which by today's standard, or pretty much any standard, doesn't sound like much, but my salary that year was $8,000.

I didn't do anything special with the money. I enjoyed living. I did things. I almost bought some real estate on the ocean in Fort Lauderdale for a meager $10,000, but I couldn't see buying some barren piece of property down on the coast. Of course, today, it is probably worth 500 times that, but then it was just a matter of living.

The 1957 World Series had been a case of two heavyweight teams proving that what wins the World Series is pitching and defense. Oh, yeah, and two fleeting legends from out of the blue that summer and fall named Bob Hazle and Nippy Jones, with many Red Schoendienst hits thrown in for good measure. They made all the difference in the world to the final outcome.

Young Joe Torre (L), now a Brave, emerges from the dugout to take pointers with the glove from still young but veteran older brother Frank. A Milwaukee water bubbler (right) is at the ready.

1958: *The Kiss of Death*

*A*S WORLD SERIES CHAMPIONS, THE MILWAUKEE *Braves were on top of the world. The people of the city of Milwaukee were ecstatic. The media were at our feet. The great young stars like Henry Aaron, Eddie Mathews, and Lew Burdette were now getting some of the media attention they deserved. Not the same magnitude of attention they would have received playing on either coast, but they were in the national spotlight at last.*

For veterans like Spahn and Schoendienst, it was about time. They were finally getting the rings, rewards, and acclaim they'd fought so long and hard for. I was more than pleased to be an integral part of such a great group of guys.

In 1958, we had pretty much the same great club, although for the season we were to drop a few more games that we had in winning the pennant the year before. But the result was the same, and we finished ahead of Pittsburgh by a full eight games. Swoons in September were distant memories.

1958 was the one season in which I played as close to regularly as I ever would. I hit .309 and struck out only 14 times in well over 350 at-bats. I started at first base from game one and Adcock played a lot of games in left field that year. Fred Haney had made the decision early on to put Adcock in left field, even though he was now over his broken leg. I had proven in 1957 that I could play the game and hit.

Adcock wasn't too excited about being in left field. But he wasn't going to bellyache, at least not yet. We had more strength defensively with me at first and the fact that I had proved that I was capable of being an offensive force with timely hits during the 1957 season and two home runs in the World Series helped Haney make the decision to keep both of us in the line-up.

Haney also decided to go with either Bruton or Schoendienst leading off and me hitting second. Playing every day and hitting in front of Mathews and Aaron was a plus because they certainly didn't want to walk me to get to them. I was not a home-run threat. I got to hit a lot of fastballs and my

When given the chance to play every day, Frank Torre was a solid batsman. A lifetime .273 hitter, he hit .270 in his years as a Milwaukee Brave, including five triples in each of the 1957 and 1958 seasons. Nearly a fifth of all his hits were doubles.

walk-to-strikeout ratio was very good. I set the table for our more productive hitters, and I got to play most of the games.

That year, I was tied for the team lead in triples most of the way. I ended up with five and Henry Aaron had four. The year before, he had six and I had five. (*Aaron racked up 14 triples in 1956.*) I did not have speed on the base paths, but I sure used to break everybody's chops about leading the team in triples. Other than a couple of guys—Aaron, Mantilla, Bruton— who were indeed fleet, we didn't have too many guys who could run great anyway.

Spahn won so many games, 22 that year, that I only wish there was some kind of a record where you could break out his career for the first half and the second half of each season. Year-in and year-out, he would be borderline .500 at All-Star

Orlando Cepeda turns his wrists on one. Cepeda hit .312 in 608 at-bats with 25 home runs in his 1958 rookie season and never looked back. A seven-time All-Star, he put up 379 home runs and 1,365 RBIs in 17 seasons.

time. Then in the second half of the year, he would win about 80 or 90 percent of his games.

We used to kid Spahnnie about it. We could never figure it out, but once he got in the groove, maybe it was the warmer weather, he was unbeatable. I mean, he would just proceed to be absolutely dynamite.

Aaron became a Gold Glove fielder in 1958 (and in '59 and '60) and hit .326 with 30 home runs. Mathews had one more homer than Henry.

Around the league, Ernie Banks lit it up for the Cubs that year and was MVP with 47 home runs, 129 RBIs and a .313 batting average in 617 at-bats. The talent around the league was awesome. Ashburn hit .350 (league leading, as well as was his 215 hit total), Musial .347 and Mays .337, while also leading the league in stolen bases. (*Mays led the league in stolen bases in four consecutive seasons—1956 (40), 1957 (38), 1958 (31), and 1959 (27).*) Orlando Cepeda also became a mighty presence that year, coming in near the top in hits and RBIs, and leading the league in doubles (38) as a rookie.

Being world champions and as young as we were, you can imagine the exhilaration we felt. As we headed onto the circuit, no place was wilder than the West Coast, where the Dodgers and Giants were now in their first seasons in the warm California sun.

It was a special time out in California. With the arrival of the Dodgers and Giants, Californians up and down the coast felt and acted just like the Milwaukeeans had back in 1953, and we were turned loose out there as World Champs.

One incident that takes the cake occurred with a couple buddies of mine who were actors in Hollywood. They were going under the names of Alan Austin and Lee Winters. This Alan Austin was the same Alan Austin who was in the foursome

1958: The Kiss of Death

Towering Gene Conley, looming over hitters from atop the mound at 60 feet 6 inches away. A three-time All-Star, Conley used his lanky frame not only to hurl major league fast balls but to play nine seasons with the Boston Celtics.

with O.J. Simpson when he played golf at the Riviera Country Club, many years later.

They had a friend by the name of Warner Tobe, who was in the movie business. I think he sort of liked men and he apparently had a liking for me. He was going to throw a party at his fancy Beverly Hills house up in the mountains. I was not concerned, because there were going to be plenty of starlets there. It was on an off day before a series against the Dodgers. I was going to take my roommate and a few other guys to the party.

Johnny Logan was my roomie at the time, but he had brought his young son along on the trip, so that eliminated him. I wound up taking Red Schoendienst, Lew Burdette, Gene Conley, and myself to this party.

It was a beautiful place, a very warm night, with a lot of people, and numerous attractive women. We got to drinking and it was very hot and the owner of the place, the host said, "Why don't you guys go swimming?" He had bathing suits for the guys and we went swimming and some of the women complained. "How come you don't have bathing suits for the women?" A couple of ladies actually jumped in the pool with their clothes on.

It seemed like everybody was having a good time and this set off a little chain reaction. People started to throw each other in the pool with their clothes on. I picked up and tossed in this one girl who was all dressed up. Just scooped her up and launched her in her fancy dress into the deep end.

Nick Adams, the actor, who got to be reasonably famous sometime after that (*The Rebel, Johnny Yuma*), was unemployed at the time, and was there with this girl. She got a little hysterical, screaming, "Oh, you've ruined my clothes," and old Nick, just a kid at the time really, started to talk tough and everything.

Seemed like he was trying to live up to some image he had in mind for himself. We started to plead with him that we'd buy her a new outfit, "We're sorry, we thought everybody was going swimming," we kept saying.

But Nick would hear none of it and Burdette got pretty much into it with the guy. After a while, Lew got tired of Adams continuing to badger us. Nick was a little bitty guy, and Lew finally said, "Look, enough is enough. If you're not going to accept our apology and you want to take this further, let's just go outside and settle this thing."

After motions to step out to the street, Adams backed off. Around that time, we felt we should leave. But right before we did, Conley, who was as strong as an ox and 6 foot 9, and played in the off-season for the Boston Celtics, picked up another young lady. He had a couple of drinks in him, and staggering a little bit with the girl in his arms, intending to send her into the pool, accidentally crashed into an antique piano. Together they fell into it and busted it into a million pieces.

Up until then, the host had handled the chaos pretty well. Even with the piano smashed, he just shrugged and said, "I was going to redecorate anyway so I might as well replace that," but he was clearly upset and we had definitely overstayed our welcome. Pretty soon, we were tipped off to the fact that someone had placed a call to the cops. Beverly Hills' finest were on the way up.

We decided to skedaddle and jumped into our car. Red Schoendienst was in the front of the car with Burdette driving, and Conley was sitting in the back with another girl we were giving a ride back to town.

Somehow Burdette and Conley got into sort of shadow boxing, and unfortunately the girl got hit and quickly developed a little bit of a mouse on her eye. As we were rolling down the hill, we saw a couple of cop cars going up.

We made our getaway, but our passenger became a bit hysterical. We calmed her down and dropped her off and then went back to our hotel.

The next day, we had a game. As we ran off the field after infield practice, a whole bunch of guys were standing in the runway of the Coliseum, leaning over each other and reading a newspaper.

It was like World War II had been declared. The headline said, "Braves Stars in Big Hollywood Brawl," and it had all our pictures plastered all over the front page.

The other guys in the incident were all married and the headlines and story made it seem a lot worse than it really was. Two things happened. Of course, the press came around and beat us up a little bit. Because I was single, I basically took the brunt of everything for the other guys. I had no problem with that.

Meanwhile, wire reports had been inflaming the folks back home and the phone lines were burning up. Fred Haney, our manager, was pretty aggravated. I was making my eight grand a year plus or thereabouts and he took me aside and said, "If I ever see your name in the society pages again, even in a gossip column, it's going to cost you $500."

When we got back to Milwaukee on our chartered plane— in those days, the airports were a little friendlier, and the players' wives and family were allowed right out on the run-way—all the wives who were greeting their husbands just moved as a group to the other side to avoid me. I was the bad actor who had caused all this, this malevolent force that had led these good husbands astray. I was on their taboo list, and they weren't going to talk to me. Especially the wives of the married guys shunned me for quite a while as the team's bad boy.

Indeed, those were heady times for young athletes wearing World Series rings. With games in Los Angeles and San Francisco, there were actors and starlets in abundance. One famous actor of the time was Jeff Chandler. He was a big Braves fan, and Warren Spahn was his favorite pitcher, but he'd never seen Spahn pitch in person.

We were playing the Dodgers and Spahnnie always had a hell of a time against them. The first time we ever played out there, they had to play in the Coliseum. (*Dodger Stadium in*

1958: The Kiss of Death

Chavez Ravine did not open until 1962.). Jeff Chandler came out purposely to watch Spahnnie pitch.

The only trouble was that Jeff showed up in the second inning and Spahnnie had already been knocked out of the ball game. We were going from LA to San Francisco to play the Giants and Spahnnie was scheduled to pitch again a few days later.

At batting practice in San Francisco an hour before the game, we hear a loud, distinct voice from up in the stands yelling out, "I'm not going to miss you today, Spahnnie." It was Jeff Chandler looking like a million bucks. He got there early, flanked with a few beauties, to make sure that if Spahn got knocked out, he was going to see it.

Our life in the fast lane extended beyond baseball. Actually, for about two of my years in Milwaukee, as one of the few

The superb Red Schoendienst, whose 200 hits (122 for the Braves) and .309 batting average in 1957 were a springboard to the Braves' championship season. Red was an All-Star in ten of his 19 major league seasons.[11]

bachelors on the club, I was reasonably well ingratiated with the local female population other than the players' wives.

Another local *bon vivant* was Paul Hornung of the Green Bay Packers. Paul's reputation as a rake was really on a whole different level than mine, but we were friends.

When Vince Lombardi arrived in Green Bay, the Packers were a truly terrible, terrible team. I think in his first year as a coach they were 1–11 or something like that, and they always played two regular season games in Milwaukee (the Packers were 1-10-1 in 1958 under Scooter Maclean. They were 7-5 in Lombardi's first year, 1959.) That gave Paul and me a chance to strut our stuff and we used to run around together quite a bit.

We had the practice of going out on Saturday nights before his Packers games and we were familiar with all the local watering holes. As two major bachelors we'd compare notes and everything, and this one time the Baltimore Colts were in for the game and we were out on the town. We connected with these two gals and we were sitting in this booth and it's getting a little past midnight and lo and behold, in walks Coach Lombardi.

Now I could see him coming in, but Paul couldn't because he's got his back to the door. Vince comes over and doesn't say a word. He just puts both hands on Paul's shoulders and Paul looks up over his shoulder and without saying a word, gets up and follows Vince out the door. I had two girls to keep company for the night.

The next morning, I was heading into the clubhouse at County Stadium. The Packers occupied the same lockers as the Braves and I wanted to wish Paul a good game. As I was going in, Coach Lombardi spots me from behind the frosted glass door of the coach's office. With a nod of his head and a forefinger aimed right at me, he summoned me inside.

1958: The Kiss of Death

"What the hell's going on out there?" a dapper Vince Lombardi wants to know, with four-time Pro-Bowler Bill Forester kneeling out of the line of fire. The legendary coach also wanted to know what his star running back Paul Hornung and the estimable Frank Torre were doing out at all hours on a Packers' game night.

Green Bay Packer Paul Vernon Hornung, the Golden Boy and 1956 Heisman Trophy winner, was a triple-threat scoring sensation (run-pass-kick), contemplating past or future conquests, on the field or off.

He got straight to the point. "I don't want you running around with my star running back on game night." I got the message.

Later that same season, I was out with Paul again, and also with Jim Taylor and Max McGee, quite a rowdy pair in their own right. Again Paul and I were with two young ladies, at a place called The Franchise. Only this time at about 11:30 p.m., Paul looks at his watch and says, "I gotta go back." And he got up and left. He took Vince very seriously.

Vince and I later became friends on the business and banquet circuit.

Even though we were the World Champions, 1958 was not all fun and games. The addition of Red Schoendienst to the club had given us a big boost the year before and now Red was a mainstay on a team defending its championship.

But sometime during the course of the '58 season, Red contracted tuberculosis. Only we didn't know it at the time. He also fractured a finger on July 4. His locker was right next to mine. Every day it would take him a little longer to get ready for a game. No one knew what the matter was. Toward the end, it got to be pretty pathetic because his legs were so discolored. I would say to him, "Red, what the hell happened? What did you get hit with?" You'd try to think if he had made a bad slide or something.

He would shake his head and get dressed for the game and say, "I don't feel real good and I get tired all the time." But what a player. That year, however, in contrast to the year before, he only played in a few more than 100 games. Felix Mantilla picked up the slack, and while Red's production was understandably off from a league-leading 200 hits (78 with the Giants before being traded to the Braves) the year before, he still came up with 112 hits, many of them doubles (23). Only Aaron hit more doubles for the club that year (34).

It was a hot summer and at first we blamed Red's condition on the weather and fatigue. But after the season, he called in and we learned that he had discovered that he had TB. While it is almost unheard of now, it was becoming quite rare even then.

Somehow Red made it through most of that year. Near the end, he began to wind down and wasn't playing much.

The next year he was almost totally out of the action. He was fighting for his life. At best, he was in bed a lot. Entertaining any thoughts of playing ball was unheard of. He came back in 1960 when it really didn't look like that would happen.

Eight-time All-Star catcher Roy Campanella hit 242 home runs in ten seasons with the Brooklyn Dodgers. A model backstop, Campy left a .988 fielding percentage working behind the plate.

If you look at Red's career, he had a few more good seasons, but never regained the form or posted the numbers he'd achieved with us in 1957 and 1958.

That's also about when Major League baseball decided that they were going to start giving players check-ups at Spring Training. Up until then, it was like a speed check. They took your temperature, your pulse, put a stethoscope on your heart, and that was your Spring Training check-up. "Get out on the

In 22 major league seasons Willie Mays hit .302, with 3,282 hits, 660 home runs, and 1,903 RBIs. A perennial National League all-star (24), and a two-time league MVP, Hall of Famer Mays led the league in runs scored once, hits once, triples three times, home runs four times, stolen bases four times, average once, on-base-percentage twice and slugging five times. Famous for his daring base running and dashing outfield play, he recorded only 141 errors in 7,431 chances, and made 7,095 put-outs. In six post-season trips, he received a World Series ring in 1954 when the Giants swept the Cleveland Indians. Center-fielders will always be measured against the play and spirit of Willie Mays.

field." But after what happened to Red, they really began to go through the exercise of checking every one of the players much more thoroughly.

In 1958, I really came into my own as a hitter. With Adcock out in left, I was playing regularly and having a positive impact offensively. For whatever reason, I loved to play against the Dodgers. But as a scrapper, I needed to take advantage of every edge I could get.

Roy Campanella, their great catcher, always gave the pitcher the fastball sign on the first pitch, in order to protect himself when his arm was leaving him. Consequently, any time the pitcher shook him off, it would always be a breaking ball. You almost always knew what was coming in Campy's latter years.

I remember one time batting second in the line-up in Ebbets Field against Johnny Podres, who prided himself on getting any one of his pitches over at any time. Hank Aaron was hitting third and now Podres has three balls and two strikes on me. There was a man on second base. You know you have to get a fastball because he doesn't want to walk you and get to Henry Aaron. Campy puts the number one down and John shakes it off. He throws a curve and I hit the ball off the scoreboard for a double.

He turned toward me at second and shouted, "How could you be looking for a curve ball?" I felt like telling him, "Shit, I didn't look for it, I knew it was coming." I think I hit about .500 against the Dodgers lifetime.

That year, the Giants made a great run at us early in the year. But by August, we started to put some distance between us. Playing regularly, it was a great season for me to compare two of the best ever, Henry Aaron and Willie Mays.

When people are gifted by the Good Lord to be superstars, they should be superstars. That's what made Willie Mays so great. He received a lot of gifts and he made up his mind early in his career that he was going to put them to use and be the greatest player that ever lived. He worked hard and became, in my humble opinion, the greatest player who ever lived.

Aaron hit more home runs and had more RBIs. Mays hit slightly better for average over his lifetime. Both were great outfielders. I think Mays gets much more credit as an outfielder in center than Aaron got playing right field. Aaron had a magnificent arm and Mays was much more of a force on the base paths.

If you ask me to compare the two, Aaron versus Mays, Hank Aaron was a great five-tool player. He could field, run, hit, throw, and think. He utilized all five tools, but not all of them equally as much as he should have or could have. As a player in Milwaukee, he played right field at County Stadium and not center field at the Polo Grounds.

The Polo Grounds had a center field of 505 feet. It was built where left and right field were close to home plate, and it was short, but there were huge gaps, creating a wide-ranging territory for whoever might be there to cover it. Because Willie was fortunate enough to be the center fielder at the Polo Grounds, he got to show off all of his abilities.

In the case of Hank Aaron, he played, though a lot of people will question me, as good a right field as anybody I have ever seen. This goes for the Clementes and Robinsons and all the other people who have been publicized like crazy. He had a good, strong, accurate arm, maybe not as strong as a few individuals who played the game, but he made up for it in accuracy. He could throw like a rifle shot.

Red Schoendienst (left), Frank Torre (14), Bob Rush (17) and Ed Mathews (41), greet Henry Aaron at the plate after one of his life-time 755 home runs.

Mays didn't have a tremendously strong arm, but he also had a great accurate arm. He too used all the tools and probably had the greatest baseball instincts of anybody I have ever seen. And I think that most baseball people would agree with me on that, even though Hank had tremendous instincts as well.

I remember a time when I was playing first and Willie came up with a man on second. He beat out an infield hit and drove the guy to third. The runner rounded third and I made a feint of a throw to the plate. Willie went for it and I tagged him out.

A year later, in almost the same situation—of course, I had no recollection of the play the year before. I came up throwing with the fake to the plate and this time, Willie hops back to the bag and says, "You didn't think you'd catch me again with that, did you?" He saw everything and remembered everything.

On the base paths, Henry could steal anytime he wanted, but he played with the Milwaukee Braves, and we were not much of a base stealing team. We were a power-hitting team and Hank Aaron was too valuable as a player on the team to turn loose except when absolutely necessary. If he stole 20 to 25 bases, that was plenty.

Actually, when I was there, he didn't steal much at all. He picked up the pace later in his career, which is kind of ironic when you think about it. Just shows how smart he was and how he continued to learn and develop as a player. He probably had as good a percentage stealing as almost anybody who ever lived. I would venture to say that he was 80 percent plus every year in terms of stealing bases (76.68 % (135th overall), first in 1966 and 1968).

Willie was faster, but not by much. Willie was also flashier. He stole more bases (338 to Aaron's 240), but he was also thrown out more (76.64% SB, 137th). The fact that he played from coast to coast when he went from New York to San Francisco brought him huge additional attention. What San Francisco lacked in size in center field, the wind more than made up for. He still had a chance to show off his wares.

If Hank had been a center fielder, though, I'm convinced he probably could have been as great an outfielder as Willie was.

As far as hitting was concerned, there's no doubt, in my mind at least, that Hank was a much better all-around hitter

"I got it." Henry Aaron simulates locating a high fly ball in the sun.

Henry Aaron takes a cautious
lead off first base behind
Gil Hodges of the Brooklyn Dodgers.

than Willie was. But somewhere along the line, maybe six to eight years into his career, he put two and two together. He realized that he was going to make more money and it was going to be more beneficial to hit home runs than to hit for average, and he changed his style, and it definitely took away from his batting average.

Early in his career, if anybody was going to break the .400 barrier, again, in my view, it was going to be Hank Aaron. He

An angular Gene Conley steps up for a spring training interview with Braves publicity manger Donald Davidson.

hit the ball all over the place and he hit it with authority, and he was a gap hitter in the early days. Therefore, for my money, Hank Aaron was probably as good a right fielder as ever lived, and Willie Mays, playing a more glamorous position, in my opinion, was the best player who ever lived.

Being considered a fine first baseman myself, I also got to take stock of my competition at the position. Gil Hodges was by far the best fielding first baseman who ever lived and deserves to be in the Hall of Fame.

He did everything so flawlessly and he did it as a right-hander. Having played against him, and considering myself one of the finest fielding first basemen who ever played the game, he'll never get the credit for the things you can't read in the statistics.

There have been a lot of good ones, Keith Hernandez and a lot of guys, outstanding defensive first basemen. But Gil was unbelievable. He covered more territory, he handled low throws, and he could make the throw to second base when they

The Braves play cards in the club house during a rain delay, Henry Aaron and Bill Bruton dealing with Ed Mathews (far right) and Frank Torre (at back) trying to follow the action.

would attempt to sacrifice somebody over or on a double play, better than anybody, and he made it look easy.

But most of the time in the newspapers, you didn't even read about it because it was expected of him, and he wasn't flashy at all. Gil was a steely spirit who helped the club win games. A true gentleman.

Playing on a world champion with every reason to think we were going to do it again also made for a lot of fun on the team. The club's publicity director, Donald Davidson, was a midget, and unfortunately for him, he was the brunt of a lot of the jokes, especially from Spahn and Burdette.

Donald used to have a specially made little motorcycle that he drove around on, and then he'd park it. I mean, it was very tiny. One time, Spahn and Burdette took it and hooked it up on a rope and cranked it up the stadium flagpole. Donny couldn't get his transportation down and it was quite pathetic. Meanwhile, these *bona fide* stars were rolling around in the grass with their sides splitting.

And of course, every other word out of Donald's mouth was a four-letter one. I remember the time in Cincinnati when we were on a road trip and we checked into the hotel about 2:30 in the morning after a grueling trip. The lobby was pretty well deserted and this hotel had a lot of floors on it. It wasn't like today when you get shown to your room. We were handed our keys and were on our own.

Donald Davidson had a room on about the 35th floor, and the floor button was high up in the elevator. We pressed our buttons and Donald was too short to press his floor and Burdette just pressed his button and refused to press Donald's floor.

We got off and he was riding up and down on the elevator so much that at 3 a.m. in the morning, he was angry enough to want to check us out of the hotel and go someplace else.

I'm sure after a while somebody gave him a break. I should have stepped in instead of leaving him to the tender mercies of Spahn and Burdette.

There was also the time about 20 minutes before a game with the stands filling fast that they lured Donald under some pretense into the outfield near the bullpen. When they got their hands on him, they held him down and removed his pants. Poor Donald had to make his way back to the dugout in his boxers in front of about 23,000 people, with the pitchers yelping and hooting from their bullpen perches.

1958: The Kiss of Death

The mighty left-hander Warren Spahn delivers. Spahn won two games and lost one in the 1958 World Series, posting a 2.20 earned run average, and striking out 18.

But you talk about somebody who had a mouth on him, Wes Covington was the only guy I've ever seen able to put Spahn and Burdette in their place. Together, they were absolutely impossible to deal with. They were like Abbott and Costello. They would destroy anybody and everybody and Wes Covington was the only individual I've ever seen who could truly shut them both up. He was very intimidating, almost like the Muhammad Ali of baseball. He had a quick mind and a quick mouth.

Even Hank Aaron had his differences with Warren Spahn. Spahn had a tendency to be very, very serious when he was pitching and much more of a jokester when he wasn't. Off the mound, he could be kind of a clown. This was very distracting to the guys who were engaged at the moment. It was just Warren's make-up. Many of us, including myself, almost laid him out more than once. You're out there trying to get a base hit or trying to win a ball game and because he's not pitching, he's basically in Never-Never Land, cutting up. He got us upset quite a few times.

Despite our ups and downs and occasional high times, again, come October, we found ourselves in the Fall Classic. This time, we opened up the proceedings on our turf. This time, we were the prohibitive favorites.

Durable Yankees right-fielder Hank Bauer led the American League with nine triples in 1957, and made three All-Star teams. His four home runs and eight RBIs in the 1958 World Series were Braves killers.

1958: The Kiss of Death

THE 1958 WORLD SERIES

GAME ONE

First game, you have Whitey Ford against Spahn, and Milwaukee wins 4 to 3. We were respectful of the Yankees, but no longer in awe of them. I was in the game but didn't start. With Whitey Ford pitching, Adcock started at first. The Yankees actually had a 3-to-2 lead after five and going into the eighth. After a scoreless ninth, we took the first one at home in the tenth on singles by Adcock, Crandall, and Bruton.

Mathews, Aaron, Adcock, and Crandall all scored, with Adcock going 2-5. Frank pitch hit and was 0 for 1. Warren Spahn was 2-4 with an RBI in his own cause. He gave up eight hits in ten innings, including two over the fence (Skowron, Bauer) and struck out six. Whitey Ford lasted seven innings

Fearsome switch-hitting Yankees slugger Mickey Mantle in his natural left-handed batting stance. Mantle was an American League All-Star in 16 of his 18 professional seasons, and a three-time league MVP. Owner of seven World Series rings, he hit 18 home runs in World Series play, hoisting a total of 536 four-baggers in his big-league career.

before Ryne Duren took the loss. Four Yankees had two hits apiece (Bauer, McDougald, Berra, Skowron). The Yankees left seven men on base, but none in scoring position.

GAME TWO

Game two, Milwaukee beats the Yankees again, to the tune of 13 to 5. Burdette versus Turley. In fact, I used a calm word. We battered Turley and Maas (Duke) for seven runs in a first inning capped by a Lew Burdette homer. With this victory, Burdette had won four straight World Series games.

I remember Lew hitting the home run and we felt fortune smiling warmly upon us. Lew wasn't as good a hitter as Spahn, but he was sort of a tough out for a pitcher. Buhl was the one who was a feeble hitter. He couldn't hit anything. Anyway, that game was pretty much over right then. We picked up more runs in the late innings. Plus, at that stage of the World Series, we felt pretty good about ourselves. Going in, we felt we had a better team in 1958 than we had in 1957, and we didn't feel the Yankees were as strong in '58 as they were in '57.

Were we cocky going into the '58 World Series? A lot was written about our supreme confidence. I think Lew had predicted that he and Spahn would repeat what had happened the previous year.

But there was a little negative pattern developing, even though we were up two games to none. In the first game, Skowron and Bauer connected on home runs, and in our second win, Mantle hit two out of the park and Bauer hit another one. The Yankee hitters were starting to find themselves and their bats were catching up with our pitching.

These consecutive World Series were also my only chance to size up Mickey Mantle up close. Mickey, even with all his problems, was definitely a superstar. Like so many Yankee

1958: *The Kiss of Death*

Yankees slugger Roger Maris, who with Mickey Mantle, enthralled a nation in the summer of 1961 as together they chased the home-run ghost of Babe Ruth. Maris broke the Babe's seemingly insurmountable record of 60 home runs in a season, with 61, but it took him 162 games, not Ruth's 154, to do it. Maris was Most Valuable Player of the American League that year with 142 runs-batted-in and 132 runs scored. He achieved All-Star status in 12 different major league seasons.

fans, you sort of dream of what might have happened if he hadn't had as many physical problems as he did. Here was a physical specimen, equally potent from both sides of the plate. He could run like the wind. He didn't steal bases (lifetime 153) because he was on the Yankees and they just didn't steal many bases. He was an outstanding center fielder, he had a good arm, but it seemed as though he was always playing hurt.

Whether it was heredity or just things that happened to him [*the famous outfield rubber drainage cover incident*][12] he was ill-fated with respect to injuries. He became a star at a young age, played on winning teams, and was in one World Series after another. Potentially he could have been the greatest player who ever lived, but a lot of things eliminated that possibility.

One thing about Mickey, and I know it's a silly thing, but when you play first base, you see all these other players at close range. Mickey Mantle was the only player I ever played against, who when he crossed first base, running out a ground ball, I could never feel his foot touching the base. Wrapped up in bandages and everything else, he glided, he was so light on his feet, I guess. I could never tell when he actually touched the base. Don't ask me why. I used to scratch my head over it. That didn't exist for Mays or anybody else. That's the thing that always stood out for me.

When Mickey batted, he had a tendency on occasion to bunt successfully with two strikes. We used to almost hope he would do it because we were sort of satisfied if he succeeded. He had worked hard on it and he was good at it, but he would do a team a favor when he bunted because he was so dangerous otherwise.

Not taking anything away from Roger Maris, but if Mickey Mantle hadn't been there, Maris would never have had the chance to break the home-run record. There's no pitcher alive who's going to walk Maris intentionally to get to Mickey Mantle. I don't know if manager Ralph Houk was real smart or lucky, or if he felt that Mantle was a better hitter so he could handle trying to be pitched around better than Maris. But the move he made, putting Maris in front of Mantle, was the key. Probably if that 1961 season had started a little better for Mickey, then *he* might have done it (hit 60 in 154 games). These are things the box scores just don't show.

People criticized Yankees teammate Billy Martin as being a bad influence and leading Mickey astray, but between Billy and Whitey, they probably saved his life a million times. The

1958: The Kiss of Death

Two-time All-Star and veteran Cub, Milwaukee Braves pitcher Bob Rush picked up 15 wins against 12 losses for the Braves in two seasons. He took one loss in the 1958 World Series.

one thing about Billy was that he drank a lot, but he could handle his liquor and he knew what he was doing all the time. He was a street-tough kid and he took care of Mickey. He kept Mickey out of trouble. Mickey didn't drink as much as people thought he drank, because he couldn't drink. He'd have two or three drinks and he'd appear like he had been drinking for a week. It affected him differently because his stomach couldn't handle it and I'm sure, just like the movie shows, there were mornings when he had a tough time answering the bell. But he always did.

Bruton and Covington led the parade going 3-4 for each, Bruton scoring twice with one RBI and Covington with two RBIs scoring once. Aaron, Mathews, and Schoendienst each also scored twice. In addition to a Bruton blast, pitcher Burdette launched a home run of his own with two men (Crandall and Logan) on. Burdette went the nine inning distance allowing the five runs on seven hits and giving up three home runs. Mantle was valiant for the Yankees with two hits in three at-bats, three RBIs, and two runs scored, including his fourth-inning home run. All five Yankees pitchers were ineffective. Loser Turley lasted only one out (a third of an inning) as did Maas, to be followed by Kucks, Dickson and Monroe. Frank was 1 for 5 with an RBI in game two.

GAME THREE

New York wins game three 4-0 at New York, Larsen beating Bob Rush. McMahon pitched two innings. I remember getting two of our six hits off of Larsen in that game (in four at-bats), but otherwise we did very little against him. Don Larsen was one of those pitchers who would lull you to sleep. You always wanted to hit against him and he was always around the plate, but he would change speeds and move the ball around and you always took the right turn when you got to first base. He always seemed to get the hitters out when he had to.

My hits were just singles. There was nothing spectacular about them. I felt pretty good about my hitting going into the Series because I had been on a good run all season long. As we say, check the records.

We were leading the Series, but it seemed the whole team stopped hitting that day. Every single one of us stopped hitting and Haney had to make a business decision regarding his pitchers.

Like everybody else, we were second guessing him, but in this Series he brought a couple of pitchers back on short rest. Even when we got ahead three games to one, there was some question whether he should have given Carlton Willey or one of the younger pitchers a start and given our heavyweights the normal rest.

1958: The Kiss of Death

Braves pitchers Bob Rush and Don McMahon fall to Yankees Larsen and Duren. While Torre and Schoendienst poked two hits each, Bruton, Aaron, Mathews and Logan were a combined 0-12 and five bases on balls among them. Duren gave up no hits in two save innings after Larsen paced the Yanks for the first seven frames, striking out eight. Bauer hammered in all four RBIs for the New York club, including his seventh inning home run with a runner on off of McMahon in the seventh.

GAME FOUR

So Spahn then pitches in game four on three days' rest. There was an off day, which was fine. Spahn was used to pitching on three days' rest because the rotation in those days was three days, and we won that game 3-0 over Whitey Ford. Warren tossed a two-hitter and stopped Bauer's 27-game Series hitting streak. Spahn had pitched a lot of good games, but that was the best one. We go up three games to one. We were feeling mighty confident.

Warren Spahn picks up the win in a two-hit shut-out gem. The Yankees left few men on base (2) because few reached (4). Ford lasted seven before he was spelled by Kucks and Dickson. Frank was 0-1 pinch-hitting. Adcock went 0-3. Spahn had a hit in four at-bats with a run batted in. He also went down swinging twice. The Braves shifted outfielders throughout the game with Aaron playing right and center, Andy Pafko playing left and right fields, Covington in left, and Bill Bruton in center field after pinch-running. Aaron's 2-4 resulted in neither a run scored nor an RBI, although he pounded a double off Ford in the second.

Warren Spahn gets the sign and goes into his windup.

GAME FIVE

This could break your heart every time you think about this whole thing, but if you're going to laugh about it, Don McMahon was my roommate and he had promised his wife that if we won the World Series, she would be allowed to buy a fur. When we went up three games to one, Johnny Logan's wife, Dottie, said she had a contact in New York to buy this fur and since we were going to win anyway, why wait until it's over? Darlene, Don's wife, proceeded to go with Dottie Logan and bought the fur.

Don at the time was my roommate, and Darlene and Don became among my dearest friends in life. When we came back to Milwaukee after losing game five, it was my turn to have my car at the airport and I had to drive them home.

They weren't talking to each other because Darlene had gone ahead and purchased the fur. Don, being pretty superstitious, felt that she was going to turn the thing around and jinx us.

"How could you do that?" he would moan. "It's bad luck."

"It has nothing to do with the outcome, that's just superstition," she would argue back defensively. "What do you think, Frank?"

1958: *The Kiss of Death*

Don McMahon in fine form warming up on the road, posted a lifetime 2.96 earned run average over 18 seasons and was a National League All-Star in 1958.

I tried to stay out of it, but had a good laugh, figuring we had nothing to worry about. I was on Darlene's side, pretty much, but it turned out maybe to be the kiss of death.

So in game five, Burdette pitches, Pizzaro came in, Carlton Willey threw an inning against Turley, who went nine, and the Yankees win, 7 to 0, getting ten hits versus our five. They broke the game open with a six-run sixth after a Gil McDougald home run.

I played the game, and like most everyone else, went hitless, because I didn't have a very good Series, other than those two hits off of Larsen, going 3 for 17 when all was said and done, but we're up three games to two and going home.

Five Braves' hits including two by Bruton against Bob Turley in nine innings resulted in no runs. Frank went 0-3 with a base on balls. Brave Harry Hanebrink was 0-1 in a pinch-hit attempt. Burdette takes his first World Series loss after winning four straight. Bruton got on base three times with his two hits and a walk. Turley himself had two RBIs in the Yankees romp. McDougald had three, including a solo home run in the third.

A glowering Carlton Willey. His best year with the Braves was his 9-7 1958 campaign, leading the league in shutouts with four.

GAME SIX

We're still confident, playing at County Stadium, and gave Spahnnie a 2-1 lead through five innings. They scratch up a tie in the sixth and it stays that way through nine. We go into extra innings. Spahn went nine and two-third innings, and McMahon a third of an inning in the tenth as New York puts two runs on the board on a McDougal homer, and singles by Howard, Berra, and Skowron. Now they're up 4-2. We're only able to put one more across, and New York wins 4-3. The Series is tied, 3-3, and it's now a one-game affair.

In the tenth, I came up to bat with the tying run at third. I hit a hump back-liner to the second baseman. I could lie and say I hit a hard line drive, but Turley, in relief, sort of jammed me a little bit. He got in on me and I hit the ball to the second baseman. We go to game seven. Memories like that stick with you.

Four Yankees pitchers combined for the win after the Braves chased Ford in the second with two runs on five hits, with Ryne Duren picking up the victory. Frank Torre goes zero for a pinch hit attempt. Aaron is valiant with three hits in five

1958: The Kiss of Death

Yankee infielders Gil McDougald and Bobby Richardson team up on a double-play against the Braves in World Series competition.

at bats and two RBIs. Spahnnie whiffs three times with a hit and an RBI in four at-bats. Covington showed up 2-4, scoring once. Four Yankees (McDougald, Bauer, Howard, Berra) had two hits each.

GAME SEVEN

Burdette pitched on just two day's rest, but he'd done that before and we won the last game of the Series the year before too. The big question was when we were up three games to one. If you were going to use a different pitcher that was the time to do it and give Spahn and Lew a little extra rest, because the Carlton Willeys and Juan Pizarros weren't exactly chopped steak. They were pretty darned good pitchers, but it's tough to second-guess Fred Haney. He had done pretty much the same thing the year before, pitching Burdette on two day's rest, but then Spahn had the flu.

Again, it was Larsen versus Burdette, and just like the year before, Larsen lasted only two and a third innings and Turley went the rest of the way. He escaped a bases loaded situation in the third, and in the sixth inning Crandall tied the game with a home run.

Still, they touched up Lew for four in the eighth. That was it. Berra slashed a double and the Yankees took a 3-2 lead after Elston Howard singled. An Andy Carey single off Mathews' glove brought up Skowron, who hit a three-run homer to left center, and we were down 6-2. The game, and our one-year reign as World Champions, ended that way.

Frank went 0-2 with a base on balls in game seven, and was three for 17 and .167 for the series. Mathews was walked three times in this game, twice intentionally. Aaron walked once but went hitless. Del Crandall cranked a home run with no one on base. The Braves left eight men stranded in the game, five in scoring position. Skowron had four RBIs including his game changing three-run home run off Burdette in the eighth. Torre, Aaron and Covington all went down quietly in the Braves half of the eighth.

Right-handed first baseman Bill "Moose" Skowron logged a career batting average of .282 in 13 seasons. His two home runs, three runs scored, and seven RBIs in the 1958 World Series against the Braves were back-breakers. Skowron left baseball wearing five World Series rings.

1958: The Kiss of Death

At the time, the Yankees were the first team since 1925 to win a World Series after being down three games to one.

There were several other sore points about this game and they had to do with errors in the field assigned to the Braves' first baseman, me. Some have called them alleged errors but they were errors and that's the way they stand in the record book.

On the first one, Yogi was on third base and the ball was tapped up the first base line. I came in and I know Burdette went to cover first base, which is the pitcher's responsibility when the first baseman fields the ball, but he assumed there was going to be a play at home plate.

I came in and picked up the ball and Yogi wasn't going home. He stayed at third so I turned and threw to first, but Lew had run by the bag. He did have the presence of mind to stop. He was basically out of position, past the bag. He turned around and faced me, and I threw him the ball and he was, if you can picture it, stretching out from behind the base.

Normally, if you cover the base, you're in front of it when you catch the ball, but thinking the play was going to be someplace else, Lew just outran it. But Lew was a very good fielder and he sort of adjusted. From behind the base he could see the runner moving towards him down the line. I threw the ball up high to avoid the runner, and it hit the heel of Lew's glove and bounced away. The throw was where I wanted it to be but they put an E3 on the board.

The second play was somewhat different because it was a bunt play, again with a man on third. It was basically a safety squeeze and I picked it up and held the man at third. I flipped it to Lew as he ran to the foul line, which you're supposed to do as a pitcher. He was running along the base line and I threw him the ball in the base line as he was running towards first base and it again hit his glove and bounced out, and again they threw an E3 up on the board.

I mean, I fielded the ball cleanly and threw it where I wanted it, but the decision of the official scorer was to give me the error. Twice. It was frustrating, but it really didn't matter. We lost the game and whether I got the errors or he got the errors, the most important thing is, we lost the game, and the Series.

I could care less other than I made the foolish mistake in the clubhouse when the media came over, of responding. They really didn't comment, they just asked, "What happened?" I replied, not complaining or anything, "I really don't know what happened. You tell me."

Now that sounds innocent enough and it really was the truth. I wasn't sure why the plays were called the way they were, and I had no excuse. If I had the plays to do over, I would have played them the same way I did. If in doing that I was credited with errors, then so be it.

That's the way I played baseball and I felt it was the right move and it was really a minor situation and I really wasn't crying. But in the papers the next day, they had the big goat horns on me. This was fine because we would have lost the game anyway, even though it didn't help the situation. Those errors weren't the difference between us winning or losing.

If we had got some base hits and done the things we were capable of doing, they wouldn't have been so magnified. What made it so disappointing in terms of letting the truth come out, is that in today's world, there certainly would have been highlights, replays, slow motion, this and that. There's no cover up, but there wasn't that technology then.

Also a little tough to explain, that winter I waited for the official World Series film to come out, and neither play showed up on the reels. I had an opportunity later to ask someone pretty high up in baseball why that was, and I got an explanation from one guy that the film pointed out how inaccurate the calls were, so they decided not to include them. Someone else said, "We didn't want to make the official scorer look bad."

Even today if you were to try to dig up that seventh game of the 1958 World Series, I'm told the tape no longer exists. I just felt that people would like to review what happened in order to judge for themselves, like normally happens in a World Series or any other classic type event. But unfortunately you have to live with it.

Of course, today, it would be unheard of. If you buy World Series movies, you see every pitch of every inning. There would have been replays from a dozen angles.

Back to the plays. When Burdette did not catch the first one, Berra stayed at third and it gave them an extra out. Both times we gave them an extra out because we held the runner. See Yogi, as I've always said over the years, is dumb like a fox. He knew I was a good fielder and he knew I was aware of the situation and he wasn't just going to give away an out, especially at home plate.

Sometimes in a situation maybe with a fast runner where you go on contact and the guy would automatically take off, there'd be a play at the plate. But in both cases, even though Yogi was not a fast runner, he was a pretty good base runner, and he didn't bite.

Though the only thing that got me somewhat angry, though it's water over the dam, was when Lew made a comment to the press in the immediate circus after the game, that "If it makes the kid feel any better, I'll take the errors." That was Burdette's comment. Now I don't need charity from anybody.

Bob Turley broke in with the St. Louis Browns. A three-time All-Star as a Yankee, he picked up a win in the 1957 World Series, and carried off the Most Valuable Player trophy for the 1958 Series with two wins and a loss in four games pitched.

Bob Turley had a banquet that winter and I really wasn't that friendly with Bob. He made a very definitive statement that on both plays, "If I was the pitcher, I would expect to be given the errors because nothing that Torre did on either play was wrong."

I will go to my grave wondering why I got charged with the errors, but what's the difference who made them? An error is an error, and neither play changed the outcome of the game. As a team, by the way, we had four errors in game six, which we also lost.

I guess it shows that for competitors, you don't give up a championship without a little bitter taste in your mouth.

We wound up losing three straight games, and that was a depressing time. In those days, I never really was that much of a drinker, but we sat in the clubhouse after the seventh game, at home, and you could say I didn't exactly enjoy that game.

After the game, we sat there, Del Rice, Eddie Mathews, several others, and me, and consumed quite a bit of liquor.

1958: *The Kiss of Death*

Journeyman Braves catcher Del Rice frames a warm-up pitch. He committed only 75 errors in 5,965 chances in 17 seasons, all but one year in the National League.

Many of Milwaukee's finest were hanging around, and surrounded by Milwaukee cops, we were commiserating.

They knew what they were doing though, those Milwaukee police. We were getting drunk and wound up giving them pretty much all of the equipment that was still lying around, whatever bats, balls, and gloves we had. I think Del gave away his catcher's equipment.

I proceeded to get pretty plastered while my brother, Joe, in his early teens, hung out in the shadows of the locker and absorbed the loss with us.

Joe waited for me in the clubhouse and watched all that drinking going on. When we finally left for the parking lot, I was, to be candid, drunk, and it was still daylight out. World Series games then were played during the day. I shouldn't have been in that condition, but within minutes, I was driving down Wisconsin Avenue, the main drag of the old burgh, at a very excessive speed, perhaps 70 miles an hour, and Joe was scared to death. He nearly shoved his feet through the floor boards before a cop stopped me.

Right away the officer knew me. He asked me something like, "Do you know how fast you were going, Frank?"

I said something like, "Pretty fast, I guess." But he was sympathetic. He turned on his siren and escorted us to my house. It wouldn't turn out like that today.

Needless to say, there were no dips in Lake Michigan that night.

Rarities

In fewer than six degrees of separation, Frank Torre faced great Yankees catcher and legendary philologist Yogi Berra in 14 games in two World Series, splitting evenly. Here the diminutive yet powerful Berra greets the diminished but prodigious and dapper George Herman "Babe" Ruth, early in Berra's career, late in the Babe's life.

Hall of Famer Paul Waner was Frank Torre's personal hitting coach during Torre's minor league stop in Atlanta. Waner hit .333 with 3,152 hits in 20 major league seasons, primarily with the Pirates but also with Brooklyn and Boston. He ended his playing career as a New York Yankee. A four-time All-Star, he was National League Most Valuable Player in 1927 (the year Babe Ruth hit 60 home-runs.)

Warren Spahn confirms the power of teammate Henry Aaron. The two Braves stars led a dynamic cast of Milwaukee Braves that included Ed Mathews, Lew Burdette, Johnny Logan, Frank Torre, Red Schoendienst, Joe Adcock, Del Crandall, Bob Hazle, Nippy Jones, Felix Mantilla and Wes Covington to the World Series championship in 1957, and the National League pennant in 1958.

Braves clubhouse manager Tommy Ferguson, resplendent in plaid, with a latter-day Willie Mays, closing out his career with the New York Mets.

Warren Spahn, the winningest left-handed pitcher of all time, and a young Joe Torre, all spiffed up as the great lefty imparts some of his experience to the up-and-coming catcher.

Braves shortstop Jumpin' Johnny Logan jokingly fields a high hop.

Braves pitcher Don McMahon gets the expedited chauffer's treatment via a swift ride into the mound on the Braves golf cart.

Cigar-chompin' Braves pitcher Bob Buhl keeps in form with off-season ritual of signing an autograph for a fan at a dinner.

Braves make hay in a rather hokey promo shot perhaps designed for the faithful in Dairyland as Felix Mantilla (left) and Henry Aaron watch Chuck Cottier take a Scythian swing. Infielder Cottier was a Brave in 1959 and 1960 with 55 hits and three home runs total for the Braves.

Ernie Johnson came to Milwaukee with the Braves from Boston. The right-hander from Brattleboro, Vermont posted a .635 winning percentage (40-23) over nine major league seasons, all but one year with the Braves. While he was handed a loss in the 1957 World Series, World Champion ('57) Johnson appeared in three Series games against the Yankees, gave up only two hits and struck out eight in seven innings, recording a 1.29 post-season ERA.

Utility fielder and St. Louis native Harry Hanebrink spent most of his 14-year professional career toiling with minor league teams. He was called up to the Braves very late in the 1957 season and was not eligible to play in the World Series that year. He spent the entire 1958 season up with the big-league club, the only one of his pro years not spent partly in the minors. (SABR) On June 15, 1958 he hit a two-run home-run in the ninth to carry the Braves past the St. Louis Cardinals in St. Louis. (SABR).

Harvey Haddix–A Perfect Game Lost

Harvey Haddix of the Pittsburgh Pirates meets the press and tries to explain how it felt to lose the greatest game ever pitched, a 12-inning perfect effort, in the 13th, on an error, a walk and a home run that was famously called a double, 1-0.

Joe Adcock rounds second base after blasting the game-winning home run. Henry Aaron, who was on first base, was already headed for the dugout without ever scoring after he saw Felix Mantilla score the winning run. Stunned Pirates absorb the sequence as it is still playing out.

Left-hander Harvey Haddix strides out of his wind-up and delivers a pitch during his 12-inning perfect game, 13-inning loss to the Milwaukee Braves at County Stadium.

Haddix gets a call pitching his 12-inning perfect game, described as "the greatest game ever tossed," at Milwaukee County Stadium, May 26, 1959.

Haddix gathers himself after losing his 12-inning perfect game on an error by Don Hoak at third base in the bottom of the 13th inning.

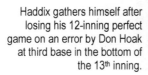

1959: *One High Hop*

O N MAY 26, 1959, AT MILWAUKEE *County Stadium, Frank
Torre witnessed what has been called the greatest game
ever pitched. Frank was relegated to the bench that
night, when Harvey Haddix of the Pittsburgh Pirates hurled 12
perfect innings, only to lose perfection when Braves infielder
Felix Mantilla reached first base on a Don Hoak error at third.
Ed Mathews sacrificed Mantilla to second, and Henry Aaron
was intentionally walked. With men on first and second, Joe
Adcock hit a home run, but thinking the game was over when
Mantilla crossed the plate, Aaron left the base paths. When
Adcock passed Aaron, Henry was called out, and Adcock's
homer was deemed a double. The final score then was 1-0, and
Haddix lost his 12-inning perfect game in the 13th.*

*Harvey Haddix pitched 14 major league seasons for five clubs
(Cardinals, Phillies, Reds, Pirates, and Orioles), winning 136
games and losing 113 in 453 game appearances, posting a 3.63
earned run average. He won 20 games in his second season,
1953, as a Cardinal. A one-time World Champion with two wins
(games five and seven for Pittsburgh in 1960), a three-time
All-Star, and a three-time Gold Glover on the mound, the
5-foot-9 Haddix was also briefly a Milwaukee Brave, purchased
on August 30, 1965 from the Baltimore Orioles, and sold back to
the Orioles just days later on September 2.*

WE WERE YOUNG. WE HAD WON ONE seven-game world championship series and lost another. The prospects at spring training
were equally as bright as they had been in 1956, 1957 and
1958.

But this time, Adcock, at spring training in 1959, basically
told them that he wasn't going to play outfield anymore, that he
wanted to play first base and he kind of pushed his way back
into the infield.

Relegated to the bench again, perhaps with a bit of an
image hangover from the sad conclusion to the Series, I also got
off to a pretty bad start, and based on that, I got to play less
and never really got back on track. I became more of a role
player again, and like I believe I had demonstrated in two
straight years, I needed the regular playing time.

I'm not flashy, but I get the job done. I seemed to have a
fair number of at-bats in the course of the year, but they were
stretched over a hell of a lot of games. Therefore, I had only one
or two at bats at a time. If you don't catch fire, you're in trouble.
It was a vicious cycle. The more I play the better I hit. The less
I play the tougher it is to get untracked. The less I play the
more importance is placed on each at bat.

I remember one streak where I went 0 for about 16 or 18,
just pinch-hitting. I'll never forget old Lou Chapman, the great
Milwaukee baseball writer. I came up three times in a row, hit
a ground ball between first and second, hit a ground ball up the
middle, and hit a ground ball between third and short, and good
old Lou said to me, "What are you doing differently now that
you've broken out of your slump?" I just got lucky and hit a
couple of balls in the hole and got base hits. Lou, God bless him,
always asked questions based on results.

1959: One High Hop

That year we had a great club, but not the total caliber of the two preceding years. We didn't win 90 games. Henry had an MVP quality year, consecutive Gold Gloves, leading the league with a .355 batting average, and leading in bases, slugging and hits, but Banks again took MVP honors on the basis of 45 homeruns and maybe a little sympathy vote for the Cubs. His numbers did not add up to Henry's.

Eddie led the league with 46 homers, and Spahn and Burdette each won 21 games. My numbers were down but this is a team sport and it all seemed very familiar.

Into July it was a three-team race between the Dodgers, Giants and Braves. San Francisco seemed to have the edge in the late part of the summer. Mays and Cepeda were lighting up the city by the bay and they had some pitchers, like Johnny Antonelli, who were winning a lot of games. But near the end of the season with the Dodgers up in San Francisco, LA swept the Giants behind Drysdale and Koufax, while we won our games and we were all breathing down each other's necks.

On the final day of the season, the Dodgers lost and we won and so we were tied for first place. We were set for a best of three playoff series. The first game was in Milwaukee and then we would head out to LA. They had flipped a coin to decide the sequence.

PLAYOFF GAME ONE

Game one, we lost 3-2 at home before an afternoon crowd. I really wasn't involved because I had been inactive for a while. I hadn't played much because I hadn't performed. We took the loss in stride, but we'd been struggling the whole streak. We weren't playing well at all, and after we lost a very tough first game, Wes Covington said he was sick, that he couldn't answer the bell for game two. Fred Haney was pretty livid. Here we'd gone scratching and Covington was one of our offensive people and now he said he wanted to go back to the hotel. Unknown to any of us, there were reasons why he was sick.

Fred Haney came into the meeting and said out loud to Covington, "If you're sick and need to go back to the hotel, I better send somebody back there with you. I'm afraid you won't find it because you haven't been there since we came to town."

Mathews, Aaron, and Adcock went a combined 0-9 with three walks. Bobby Avila playing second base and Bill Bruton drive in the Braves two runs. The Braves strand eight. Logan is 1-3 and scores. Crandall is 2-4 and scores. Frank Torre goes down in his single pinch-hit at bat. Carlton Willey goes six innings and takes the loss. The Dodgers usual suspects, Gil Hodges is 1-3 with an RBI, John Roseboro 1-4 scoring and driving in a run, Charlie Neal 3-5 with a run scored, Wally Moon 1-4 with a run scored, and Norm Larker 3-5 with an RBI. Larry Sherry pitched seven innings in relief of Danny McDevitt for the win.

PLAYOFF GAME TWO

Much to my surprise, when I showed up for game two of the play-offs, not only was I playing, but also Don Drysdale was pitching for the Dodgers, and I was batting fourth in the line-up. This was a pleasant surprise because I figure here is the season in a nutshell. If I had a good second game, maybe I'd get a chance to play in the third game of the playoff. If I did well there and had a good Series, maybe memories would be short and I'd be back in good stead with everybody.

Well, the first time up, it was almost like a blueprint that I laid out. I got up with men on second and third base, Mathews and Aaron, and I was lucky enough to get a base hit off

Drysdale. I knocked in two runs and we went into the ninth inning leading 5-2.

They managed to tie up the game in the ninth five to five and we went into extra innings. We had a lot of chances to score more runs in the ball game, but didn't. There were opportunities a couple of times during the game where different hitters had chances to break it open and they weren't able to do it.

Going into extra innings, Felix Mantilla was playing shortstop because Logan got hurt during the game.

Felix was an outstanding young ballplayer. He had good brains and knew the game. So they got a man on second base with one out and the one thing that stands out clearly in my mind was that one of their slower guys was running, Gil Hodges on second base, and Carl Furillo hit a ground ball behind second base. Felix made a really good play on the ball but he made a bad throw to first base, into the dirt in front of me. Being sensitive to the winning run now going to third, my goal was just to stop the ball and keep it in front of me.

We were essentially playing on a converted football field in the Los Angeles Coliseum, and the dirt was really not baseball dirt, it was more like hard sand. Normally when a ball hits off the dirt like that it would take a reasonably consistent hop and it would stay within range if you didn't catch it. You could at least block it with your body.

This particular ball was thrown into the Coliseum's so-called dirt, and it bounced. Now I'm six foot three inches tall and the ball bounced directly over my head and away into the stands. The game was over because the man at second who was now going to third proceeded to score as the ball bounced away.

It was a very helpless feeling because in a matter of seconds, the year was over. The unfortunate part about the situation was that with game two in our back pocket, we had

Bob Buhl ready to pitch the third game, and if that doesn't turn you on, the fact that Bob Buhl had pitched six times and had beaten the Dodgers six times that year, sure meant a lot to us.

That was in effect the end of the Braves championship era. That was really it for me with the Braves as well. We went from having a strong chance of being good enough and coming close to being in the World Series four straight years, and where they start mentioning you as one of the so-called dynasty teams, to being also rans. The Braves deservedly belonged in the same breath with the Yankees and others for discussion purposes, but a dynasty we were not, as we slipped away into the sands of time.

Both teams used every available resource going for the win, with the Braves putting a combined 22 players on the field and the Dodgers 20, the Braves fielding five different pitchers and the Dodgers six. The Braves used Burdette, McMahon, Spahn, Jay, and Rush. The Bums used Drysdale, Podres, Churn, Koufax, Labine, and Williams. Bill Bruton for the Braves went 0 -6. Mathews and Aaron each went 2-4 with Mathews scoring twice and Aaron once. Logan scored once going 1-3 and Crandall crossed the plate with one hit in six trips. Frank Torre was 1-3 with three walks and two RBIs. Gil Hodges was 2-5 scoring twice. Charlie Neal scored twice going 2-6, and Wally Moon was 3-6 with a run scored and an RBI. Braves starter Burdette surrendered five runs on ten hits through eight innings. Bob Rush took the Braves loss and Stan Williams the Dodgers win.

1959: One High Hop

Ed Mathews and Henry Aaron proudly display their league leading hitting awards from the previous (1959) season. Mathews presents his Mel Ott Memorial award as the National League's leading home run hitter that year, with 46. He also led the NL in homers in 1953 with 47 in his second season. The Mel Ott award for the annual NL home run champion was instituted in 1959, making the Braves third baseman its inaugural recipient.

Aaron here holds the John A. "Bud" Hillerich commendation and silver bat as 1959's batting champion. He racked up a .355 batting average with 223 hits, 39 home runs, 116 runs scored and 123 RBIs. Aaron also was the National League batting champion in 1956, hitting .328. Mathews and Aaron rank as the greatest home running hitting duo of all time, slugging 1,267 home runs between them, with 863 of those coming as teammates. Ruth and Gehrig hit 1,207 home runs combined overall and 859 while teammates. Mays and McCovey hit 801 four-baggers as teammates and 1,181 overall. Mantle and Maris hit 419 home runs as teammates and 811 overall.

Frank Torre's nemesis, Milwaukee Braves Manager Charlie Dressen, one fine day in the bowels of Wrigley Field, put a crimp in Frank's major league career, shipping him off to the minor leagues. As a player, Dressen hit .272 in eight seasons. Over four decades he managed five clubs, including the Dodgers to pennants in 1952 and 1953. But in 1951 his Dodgers collapsed, giving up a 13.5 game lead to the Giants, and the famous Bobby Thomson home run shot heard around the world. In 16 years as a manager Dressen won 1008 games and lost 973.

Chuck Dressen (7) makes a point to (from left) Andy Pafko, Dave Jolly, and Don McMahon.

1960: **Sideways**

O NCE *CHARLIE DRESSEN TOOK OVER AS manager of the Braves after the 1959 season that basically was the kiss of death, not only in terms of Frank Torre, but also the kiss of death for the good teams in Milwaukee. —Frank Torre*

If I have not been entirely candid up until this point, let me begin now. Maybe this classic story conveys how we all came to feel about Dressen. When he came over to the Braves as manager, it was always, "the Dodgers this and the Dodgers that," and a little of that was ok, but a little of that also goes a long way.[13]

Warren Spahn, in one of our first team meetings, one of the greatest pitchers of all time and the winningest left-hander in all of baseball, was really trying to improve himself and get along.

In a team meeting, he raised his hand and asked Dressen a question. Warren always did have trouble with the Dodgers. Very sincerely, Spahn asks, "Charlie, I've had a hell of a time trying to beat the Dodgers all these years, so maybe with all your knowledge and background of being with those guys, maybe you can tell me how to pitch them."

Charlie, gracious fellow that he was, in front of the whole team, said, "Well, Spahnnie, I can tell you how to get them out, but you don't have the stuff to do it."

You have to understand the clubhouse atmosphere. In a sophomoric way it was really funny, but not to Spahnnie. Over the years, Warren had not been able to beat the Dodgers much, and he was sincerely trying to get the inside scoop on them.

As unpopular as Dressen wanted to make himself, some of the old club hi-jinx continued. Even though Covington could back down Spahn and Burdette, they were just waiting for a chance to get back at him.

One time, Dressen held a meeting specifically about cutting out the horsing around, no doing this and no doing that. It was like waving a red flag at those guys.

Covington always was a finely attired three-piece-suit man, and often wore a fancy hat. Apparently, there had been some tampering with Wes's duds, and Dressen specifically said, "And I don't want anybody messing with Wes's clothes."

Well, we proceeded that day to go out and play the Cardinals and got beat 12 to nothing. We got killed and we were embarrassed. We were all shuffling onto the bus to go back to the Chase Hotel and in the back are Spahn and Burdette with a broomstick and on top of the broomstick is Wes Covington's very expensive hat.

Just as Chuck Dressen gets on the bus, with Covington right behind him looking for his hat, our two leading pitchers put the thing to flame. There they were standing in the back of the bus with this broomstick and Covington's hat on fire. Covington looked like he could have shot someone and Dressen, when he got excited, sputtered and spit all over the place.

That's how much respect and authority Chuck had with the Braves.

Needless to say, he was not popular at all. In fact, he was hated. Near the end with Dressen, guys were almost hoping to lose to get rid of him. A lot of people quit on him.

For me, the end came sometime in July before a game in Chicago. Admittedly, I was having a pretty miserable summer, with only 21 game appearances, 44 at-bats, and nine hits, batting .205. It was the same cycle as the year before. I didn't play regularly and so I wasn't hitting well.

Dressen called me in and shut the door and told me I was being sent down to AAA Louisville. It sort of took my breath away. For one thing, I had four and half years in the Major Leagues and you needed five for the pension plan.

I basically showed very little reaction or emotion, not wanting to give "Chuck" his satisfaction. I drove back up to Milwaukee before the game to gather my belongings.

I had several days to report to Louisville. Buddy Selig, as I recall, loaned me a car for the ride to Kentucky. I didn't go directly southeast and kind of meandered on my way. One time, I had a flat tire and had to call Bud asking him where the damned spare was, since it was one of those new deals at the time with the spare hidden under the body of the car. You could have fooled me.

You think about a lot of things on a drive like that. Looking back at it now, I'd have to say I made a very big mistake after the 1958 season. I had hit .309. Birdie Tebbetts had taken over as General Manager and there was a lot of talk about how I would be impossible to sign because I had this great year. There had been trade talk about me in the past when I really wasn't doing much. This time, I was in enough of a position of strength where I could still force the issue over my brother Joe, such that they honored their agreement to bring him into the Instructional League.

Tebbetts still had Adcock on the club and by then, Joe was balking like hell about playing left field. He really didn't want any part of it.

A few clubs were seriously interested in me, Baltimore being one. Looking back, despite the joy of playing with a winner in Milwaukee, I really should have pushed to get myself traded. Not being a flashy player, I had to play every day to really show myself off. When we went back to platooning and I became a role player again, I didn't accomplish much in that last year and a half.

Even more than that, there is the simple love of playing the game, the desire to be on the field, to get your swings and help influence the outcome.

I chose to stay with the winner and I paid for it after that year. The next season I went to spring training and I was almost back to where I started from, even though I had hit .309, and despite the fact that Birdie Tebbetts took about five minutes to sign me by giving me what I wanted.

Consequently, I played out my string, took my lumps from Dressen and it was "Louisville, here I come." My old running buddy Paul Hornung hailed from Louisville and it wasn't football season. He was home and he must have known I was headed that way by reading the papers. I finally arrived at the

hotel and I was shown to a pretty nice suite. When I opened the door, Paul was there with some drinks and a naked girl. "Where

Birdie Tebbetts caught for 14 years, all in the American League with Detroit, Boston and Cleveland. Accounted a fine defensive backstop, he hung up a .983 fielding percentage and was a league All-Star four times. He managed the Braves to 98 wins and 89 losses in 1961 and 1962, stepping in from the General Manager position he held in the previous several years.[14]

you been?" he wanted to know. "This is Sally, and she's been waiting for you."

I spent a lot of the rest of the summer traipsing around with Paul at the track and all around town. He knew everyone down there and as a Heisman trophy winner from Notre Dame, got a lot of attention wherever he went.

A new face to me at Louisville was a young catcher, an apparent defensive specialist, named Bob Uecker. Uke was there specifically to catch this young knuckleballer, Phil Niekro, who was warming up to go into the ballgame. We had a trainer by the name of Harvey Stone. The bullpen in Louisville was very close to the dugout, and somebody was screaming. "Come down, Harvey! Come down to the bullpen." Uecker had been hit with a knuckle ball. Harvey said out loud, "Oh hell, if he's hurt bad enough, he'll come over here."

Older brother Frank (right) back in a Braves uniform to support budding star and younger brother Joe Torre.

A young, un-weathered Phil Niekro, the great knuckle-baller, came up in the Braves organization, first in Milwaukee, with 21 of his 24 major league seasons twirling in Atlanta. A 300 game winner (318-274), Niekro won more than 20 games twice, recorded 3,342 strikeouts, was a five-time All-Star and is in the baseball Hall of Fame.

Then I see Uecker shuffling over with his finger hanging off because he got hit on the edge of the glove, and I'm thinking to myself. "This is some outfit, if this is the guy they got to catch the knuckleballer."

Uecker was there in Louisville and so was Moe Drabowsky. Our home games were played on the Fairgrounds, where they held the State Fair. During one home stand, the State Fair was going on and all these farm animals and displays and rides and booths were very close by. There was an amazing livestock area with sheep, horses, pigs, and cattle.

We used to have what you would call this hot analgesic stuff for the athletes to rub on their bruises and sore bones. The cream was so hot that if it was cold out, some guys would put it on their backs or their arms and it would literally burn.

Drabowsky and Uecker got this brainstorm and they took huge jars of this stuff, along with some big tongue depressors, I mean, the extra-long ones, and they crawled through the corral into where the bulls were and they took this hot stuff on these sticks and they put it under the bulls' balls and all over the place.

1960: Sideways

"I know it's up there somewhere." Comedic catcher, Hall of Fame announcer, life-time .200 hitter, and famous friend of Frank, Bob Uecker, locates a foul ball while on active defensive duty.[15]

They came back to the clubhouse and looked like they had been in a war, they were so filthy dirty with straw in their hair and everything else. I said, "Hey, what the hell is going on? Guys, what did you do?"

They're just smirking and saying, "You'll find out, you'll find out." Well, in a matter of about a half hour, we're out on the field, and at first there was all this smoke, dirt, and sand being kicked up out over behind the fence, and then screaming, yelling, and kicking across the way.

Those bulls had gone crazy, absolutely crazy. The prevailing authorities had to empty the stands and even fire trucks appeared, because this stuff had worked its magic and taken effect and it just burned up those bulls, really setting them off like, well, wild bulls and creating a clear and present danger.

It was such a commotion and nobody really knew how or why it happened except a few of us who were chortling into our gloves. It was a good thing no one got hurt, except for a few

Right-hander Moe Drabowsky found himself in Milwaukee for one of his 17 seasons, taking two losses for the Braves that year.

Frank in a Phillies uniform, where in 1962, he hit .310 in 168 at-bats.

prize show bulls with burning balls. That was Uecker and his sidekick Drabowsky.

Friends like these helped ease the sting and I had a pretty good rest of the season down in Louisville. I think I hit a solid .280 and went about the business of trying to fight my way back into the big leagues.

1960: Sideways

Prior to an extension of the right field bleachers at Milwaukee County Stadium, grandstands up on Veterans Administration Hill overlooking the stadium allowed fans to watch the Milwaukee Braves and Green Bay Packers from on high, with their view of the game from center to left fields obstructed.

The legendary voice of the Milwaukee Braves, broadcaster Earl Gillespie makes an award presentation to (from left) Del Crandall, Henry Aaron, and Joe Adcock, with Ed Mathews on deck.

Ace of Hearts

YOU BRING IT TO A MOVIE PRODUCER and he'd kick you out. The New York Yankees, managed by my brother, Joe Torre, were about to clinch a come-back win in the 1996 World Series against the Atlanta Braves, less than 24 hours after I received a heart transplant.

The Yanks had dropped the first two games at Yankee Stadium and then stormed back to win three straight in Atlanta. All the while this was going on, I was in the hospital, stable but essentially dying of congestive heart failure and waiting for a heart transplant. I'd been waiting about 80 days when the Series began.

Heading into the Series, Joe was now officially the one person in the entire history of major league baseball to play the greatest number of games without winning a championship. If it was gnawing away at him, he wasn't showing it.

I remember conversations at that time with different people and, in my own mind, after the great year my brother had with the Yankees (92-70), taking the pennant by four games and turning the American League on its head, we were just hoping that he'd win one game now in the Series and not embarrass himself and ruin the whole year.

I even had a conversation with Yankees owner George Steinbrenner, who basically felt the same way. In the meantime, Joe told both George and me, "Don't worry. I'm lucky in Atlanta and I'm going down there and we'll win three straight."

Nobody will really know whether he believed it in his heart or not. I personally thought he was on some kind of foreign substance, but the Yanks went down to Atlanta and took the first and then the second game. The affair was now tied up at two games apiece.

Naturally, everybody and his mother knew it was coming back to New York. When the team left New York down two-zip, nobody really wanted tickets for prospective games six and seven. The prevailing sentiment was that the Yankees would lose the World Series in Atlanta.

Then Joe's Yanks grabbed a third win in that oven of a stadium down there[16], with the heat-crazed moths flying around under the stadium lights and Ted Turner and Jane Fonda doing their silly tomahawk chop.

Atlanta was in shock and New York went crazy. Now New York was up in the Series three games to two, and the streets were alive with the sound of music.

The very next night, I received a new heart in a miraculous transplant operation, and less than 24 hours after that, my brother Joe was managing the New York Yankees in game six of the World Series with a solid shot to take the crown.

On this night, a lifetime of effort and dedication for Joe could culminate in a championship. He and the Yankees could get the monkey off their backs. He'd never won one, not in nearly 40 years of donning a ballplayer's garb—Braves, Cardinals, Mets—or as a manager—Mets, Braves, Cardinals, Yanks, and the Bronx team hadn't savored a championship season since 1978—and for the New York Yankees—that is some dry spell.

So Joe would become a World Champion, Series ring and all, a mere 39 years after I had been fortunate enough to win a Series ring as first baseman with the 1957 Milwaukee Braves.

We had also achieved our final victory in that now distant, glorious year, in Yankee Stadium, dropping the Yankees in a seventh game.

Now here I was, watching it all on national television, propped up on pillows, oxygen tubes spiraling out of my nostrils, surrounded by doctors and family, fully wired to a battery of monitors, media trucks lined up outside, a big but reluctant part of the story, with a new heart beating gratefully inside this 64-year-old chest cavity.

The story of how I had been fortunate enough to land in one of the world's great hospitals, Columbia-Presbyterian, in New York, with a failing old heart, was a long and arduous one. Now with a young, pulsing new model and all the attendant hoopla of a brother steering the New York Yankees, it was a testament to a lot of great people, including Joe.

Initially, I told Joe I didn't have the strength or energy to travel from Florida to New York. That is how bad it had become. I felt the Florida doctors were slowly killing me, and I didn't think I'd survive a trip north.

But eventually I had no choice. I told Joe, "I'll go to New York, providing you can guarantee me that I won't have to be examined as an outpatient. Otherwise, I don't have the energy. I need to be admitted to the hospital when I arrive, and whatever tests they're going to do, they do to me as a patient in the hospital."

Thanks to Cy Berger's nephew, Craig Evans, who worked at Columbia Presbyterian, Joe was able to arrange it. I was so debilitated and run down that my sister Rae had to travel to Florida and fly back with me to New York. I was extremely weak and not capable of flying by myself. Basically, I was a wheelchair patient.

When I got off the plane, Joe was shocked to see the condition I was in. I wasn't panicked, but I felt like the world was closing in on me. I guess that was the shadow of death. Even at the airport, I kept saying to my brother, "Get me out of here, get me out of here."

When I finally arrived at Columbia Presbyterian, he had arranged for a team of doctors to meet me, and it was the most impressive thing I'd ever seen, especially after barely surviving the medical swamps of Florida.

Here were all these experts in their related fields, all waiting for me. Each one had my file under their arm. You could tell by the questions they were shooting at me that they had actually read the files and knew everything about me.

Before I even arrived at my room, they had conducted a number of tests, poking me, prodding me, pulling blood. It was an entirely new feeling after the horrors I had experienced in Florida. Here, I sensed a new dedication and professionalism and felt progress almost immediately. I knew I was in the care of the best.

Over the next two days, they continued to give me a battery of tests and actually identified my problem, which had somehow eluded Florida's finest. I had congestive heart failure, pure and simple. Knowing this for sure and so quickly, made me even more frustrated. I immediately thought back to all the pain and aggravation I had undergone over the previous couple of years in Florida. The quacks down there had never even come close to surmising the cause of my difficulties.

In the meantime, much permanent damage had been done to my heart. As a result, it wasn't pumping enough oxygen to the rest of my body. The type of medicine and care I had been getting in Florida had just been accelerating my problem. I was growing weaker and weaker with each passing day and when I first checked in to the New York hospital, I had very little pulse. I was a physical basket case.

In order to stabilize me in New York, they began feeding me intravenously. Although my body and heart were so damaged and not getting enough oxygen, this special intravenous medicine—I called it a magic potion—was supplementing my heart. It quickly accomplished the critical act of generating more oxygen throughout my entire body.

It made me feel so much better that I could actually eat a meal, taste it, and enjoy it for the first time in months. I was in little or no pain, despite the fact that when I first arrived, they only gave me about three months to live.

I was in such rough shape that they determined they were going to try different things on me and this medicine was one of them. Fortunately, my body didn't reject it, and as long as my body didn't reject it, they could keep me alive and keep this oxygen going through my body.

But the fun had just begun. Quickly they reached the conclusion that I needed a heart transplant. When you first hear that they need to cut your heart out, it knocks the wind out of your sails. It's like the end of the world. Probably the only time gloom and doom set in for me was when they told me I needed a transplant.

Unless the rules have changed in the last few years, the age limit to get on the transplant list is 65. You have to pass an inspection in a total sort of way before you reach that age. Otherwise, they really don't want to waste a heart on someone over that age. It sounds cruel except that for everybody who gets one, there are four or five people who don't. There's a tremendous shortage. They try to give hearts to the people who will last the longest and with the most potential to live longer, healthier lives.

I have to be honest. I was pretty devastated by the whole thing. But at Columbia Presbyterian, they are very good at what they do. I already knew that. They had found my problem quickly, given me the right treatment, and had me stabilized.

They began to deal with the psychology of my situation. They started to bring people in to see me, recent transplant patients. One person might have had a heart transplant a couple of weeks before, someone else months ago, and another individual a few years before. Everybody was normal and healthy and from all different age groups, and all were lifting my spirits.

Eventually, I started to get pretty excited about the possibility of being able to live again. Now came the next kicker —I had to pass the next big inspection, and this was a very big deal. They needed to check out the rest of my body to see if I was an appropriate candidate for a new heart. They asked me if I had ever taken any drugs, and fortunately for me, I never had. Any extensive drug use anytime during your life almost completely eliminates you.

My advice to people is that if you value your long-range plans in this world, you might seriously consider what type of stimulants you deal with. For whatever reason, serious drug use, whether legal or not, eliminates you from the list for possibly receiving a new heart.

Thankfully, they never asked me if I had ever hung out with Bob Uecker.

The physical investigation of my body and detailed medical history, beyond what they conducted when I first arrived, was exhaustive. They checked out my liver, my kidneys, check you for cancers, my brain, my nervous system, things all over the place. They asked me if I had ever had this or that infection.

They even checked out my bones, creaky, gnarled, and previously broken as some of them were.

Some of the tests stretched out over quite a bit of time. I waited between ten and fifteen days for the results. These were literally the longest days of my life, because now I had gotten a little excited about living.

By the time the results came in, I just assumed I had no chance. I'm no defeatist, but at my age and having lived a full life, I felt I had to imagine some reason for them to reject me. I had smoked cigars all my life and had sustained a lot of wear and tear. You figure there's got to be something wrong with you. They really take you apart from head to toe and inside and out, and by the time they were going to tell me about it, I had considered myself dead.

While I was waiting, they kept parading in these successful heart transplant patients. They did a sensational job of providing printed matter, too. You're not much in the mood to read it, and then all of a sudden, these strangers with strong hearts were walking into my room. You know, it's "Hi, I'm Joe Blow. I had a heart transplant six months ago. Here, read this. Life's gonna be grand."

The more time that went by and the more I learned about the potential of the new heart, the more excited I was about living. But the more excited I got, the less chance I felt I had to survive.

Up until then, I had been so sick and in so much pain that I reached a point where I didn't give a damn about living that way anymore anyway. You wind up saying, "The hell with it. If this is living, then let me get the hell out of here."

Now, all of a sudden, with the stimulants they were giving me through my arm to supplement my weak heart, I was feeling lots better. Seeing people who actually had new hearts living normal lives gave me much greater desire to live. I got pretty damned excited that maybe there was a chance for me to live a normal life. The one thing I'm not is afraid of dying. But one thing that everybody should have and I especially want is to really live while I'm alive.

I remember hearing Arnold Palmer say one time, and I really didn't understand what he meant then, but he just said one simple line: "Live while you're alive." I had experienced a few years now where I was technically alive, but I hadn't been living.

Frankly, I didn't think there was a Chinaman's chance in the world that I would pass those tests.

I was a very happy man, then, when after about 12 days, I received word from my cardiologist that I had passed. I was now to go on the long list of those around the nation who were waiting for a new heart.

I was ecstatic and grateful. It was a miracle that I had passed the inspection, especially after the damage that had been done in Florida.

Now it was just a matter of hoping that my system didn't start rejecting the medicine they were feeding me until a new heart arrived. I was feeling good for the first time in years. Now it was a battle against the clock. I was living on the magic potion, comfortable, in no pain, and I had a lot of time on my hands.

It was still July and the Yankees were in the thick of a pennant race. In the ensuing weeks, I spent hours following the team, communicating with my brother, watching a few games, and listening to the rest on the radio. In the hospital I didn't have the luxury of cable television. It was a throwback to the old days. I closed my eyes and imagined the plays on the field as they unfolded.

Following Joe as he tried to manage this team to his first World Championship took my mind off my predicament. Being fed intravenously, I was pushing this little cart around all the time and making sure the knot on my gown was tied in back so my old Italian butt wasn't flashing down the corridor.

I developed survival rituals. At this stage, my spirit was back and I wanted to live. I asked my doctor what I could do to improve my chances. She talked about constant exercise, good circulation, and keeping upbeat. Victory was going to be a state of mind, patience and perseverance.

As the pennant race heated up, publicity and media opportunities were coming our way. *"Brother of Yankees manager awaits new heart in fight of his life,"* was the regular headline. The doctors and hospital PR department asked that if my heart could handle it, would I do interviews and help make the world more aware of organ donation. It would not only help my chances of finding the right match, but it would increase the chances of all the other people out there waiting for hearts, livers, and kidneys.

You bet I was interested in helping as much as I could stand. I'd always been both open and wary of the press, but now I became a media animal. Joe's approach with the Yanks was instructive. He was always available and patient with the press. As manager, he felt it went with the territory and he owed it to the fans.

There were days when I actually did six or eight interviews, whether on television, radio, or over the telephone. In order to keep my sanity and make sure I wasn't overdoing it, each morning, I'd take an exercise trek and push my cart around the hallway. They're always waking you up in the hospital anyway, so, what the heck, I felt, I'd get up early and go do a few laps.

In fact, the sight of me tooling around the corridors got to be such a popular happening in the hospital that my neighbors were instructed to clear out when I was coming through. I could walk for a mile pushing this thing around every morning at six o'clock. It was always after they woke me up either to take blood, my blood pressure, or my temperature, but before breakfast.

Still, there was a lot of time to pass. I never was much of a daytime television person. The newspapers were delivered to my hospital room first thing in the morning. I gobbled up the sports first. On the tube, there were certain programs that I liked, like *Regis Philbin* and *Seinfeld*. At 11 o'clock each morning, I watched *The Price is Right*. I never was much interested in the soaps. I would read either a book or the newspapers, and then have visiting hours and interviews in the afternoon.

Every other day, my sister Rae would drop in. We kept visitors down to a minimum—just close friends—and even they were limited. With all the news coverage, things had the potential to just get too crazy. With the press, we tried to consolidate the interviews into a couple of hours every day other than special situations. I managed to keep busy and focused.

The evenings on game nights were more difficult, but here again, I had certain shows to tide me over. I tried to walk at least twice a day, the one time seriously and the other times just to loosen my bones or maybe go sit down the hall. I couldn't leave the floor.

While there was no pain, I did suffer from occasional dizziness, probably from overdoing it, and my blood pressure would get either too high or too low. Otherwise, I was fine. For the most part, the hospital and the people who were treating me were like well-oiled machines. They kept me moving and upbeat.

I spent a lot of time being cheerleader for all the other people on my floor waiting for hearts. There were always eight or ten of us. Not all were as positive or hopeful as I was. Once in a while, we'd go visit the children's ward if they made special arrangements to hook me up, monitoring my old and decrepit heart.

When my brother came up, as often as he could during the pennant race, we would meet some of the sadder cases, the serious ones, the people who needed cheering up, and a lot of children. Maybe he'd bring an autographed ball or a hat or a picture or a jersey. You tried to do things not only to benefit yourself, but also to benefit the people around you.

After a while, the eyes and ears of the world were on me and my situation. I was very lucky to be getting the kind of attention that I was. But I also became very sensitive to the people who weren't as lucky as I was. You try to cheer them up as best you can.

Sometimes Joe and I visited kids the doctors told us for whatever reason wouldn't be around next week. You'd go in there and look at them, and you couldn't believe what you saw, they looked so healthy, some of them. But there was something going on that was going to kill them before anything more could be done for them. Of course, even today, the technology and the prognosis for the children seem not to be as advanced or positive as they are for adults, for whatever reason, and that's why it is so terribly important to accelerate pediatric research and development.

So, being involved in these ways would take my mind off of my own problems, for a lot of reasons. Number one, it didn't help to feel sorry for yourself, and second, there were a lot of people out there with problems far worse than mine.

Looking back, out of the dozen or so people also waiting, all received new hearts. I kept close track. They were my mates. Unfortunately, one person is dead now (2001). He was two doors down and got his new heart about the same time that I did. I never knew the details of his specific problem, but apparently they discovered complications. He recovered, in a sense, quicker than I did. In very short order, he was playing golf and everything. His ultimate demise had nothing to do with the cost of treatment or finances. He was a very well-to-do individual. He just very suddenly passed away. That concerned me. I checked with my doctor then and asked, "Is that what I have to look forward to?" Because this other fellow looked and felt so great and then all of a sudden, "boom," he was gone.

My doctor didn't go into the details, but she did say there were other issues and problems and they basically knew that it might happen.

I guess that what happens sometimes is that after you get the new heart for whatever reason—and I am not a medical person—other conditions crop up. These can create another set of problems that have to be dealt with. Sometimes, even though people have all the right things going for them, they just don't make it.

The transplant operation itself had come a long way in a short time. Twenty years prior to my heart operation, of the first 12, 13 operations, many people died within three weeks. I have been known to gamble a bit, and those were not great odds. But those were courageous people whose sacrifice made success possible for the rest of us. As a result, there has been a tremendous advancement and development of techniques.

For instance, now they do post-op biopsies every so often. Too many times in the past they found that people felt good and looked good and on the surface, they were fine. But there was activity going on in and around the heart that was not good. By doing the biopsies on a pretty regular basis when you first have the transplant, they discover problems that can be dealt with, providing they catch them early enough.

With my positive new outlook, I didn't doubt now that I would last to get a new heart. I really didn't think about it. This was a waiting game and there was no such thing as a sure thing, but the last thing I wanted was to be anything but positive.

The only time I started to get a little restless and antsy was right toward the end, because you just really don't know. There were a few false alarms, where they say there was the possibility of a heart, and then something would go wrong. Maybe the match wasn't just right or maybe somebody jumped up in front of me who needed a heart more than I did. Maybe they found something else wrong with the donor that made their heart not quite good enough to give to somebody else. So many factors went into it. I did have quite a few dreams where I was getting a new heart, only to wake up and realize it was all a dream.

I waited 91 days. Not that I was counting, but I certainly did figure it out after it was over. The one thing I didn't want to get into was counting the minutes, counting the hours, counting the days.

The team of heart specialists who actually conducted the surgery were definitely "A Team," because every team is the A Team; I certainly was in good hands.

You're never really given any notice and they warn you way in advance that usually the heart becomes available during the night. What happens is, most frequently, an accident has occurred. Something tragic has to take place for a good heart to become available.

I can close my eyes and pretty much remember the whole incident. It was as though a couple of people sat down and wrote a script—it was so real and dramatic, the timing of it, that I can envision it unfolding again right now.

Summer had passed into fall. Joe's team down two games had indeed swept three in Atlanta, and Joe finally had a shot to win it all.

First had come the two quick losses, but as Joe had predicted, bam, the Yanks won two, and then three in Atlanta, and all of a sudden, not only were they back in it, New York had the upper hand in its own ballpark.

After the first two Yankee wins, I started taking a lot of phone calls from people looking for tickets to games six and seven back to New York. The whole thing was surreal. Game five in Atlanta, for instance, with Andy Petitte pitching for the Yankees, was an absolute nail-biter. It was a 1-0 ball game and a lot of strange things happened.

My brother could have been second-guessed left and right. In the ninth inning he actually let Petitte go up and hit for himself—in a 1-0 ball game. He had one of the premier closers waiting in the bullpen. The game finally ended 1-0. As an individual with a weak heart, being fed intravenously to keep me going, I felt exhausted. It took me a couple of hours to unwind after the ball game and I finally fell asleep.

About 3 o'clock in the morning, my phone rang. I almost didn't answer the phone, in sort of a daze. The woman on the other end says, and I will try to repeat it exactly, "We have found a heart for you. We think it's a perfect match. Now get ready because we have to take x-rays and blood," and she hung up.

That was the extent of it. The entire conversation couldn't have been more than ten or fifteen seconds. Initially, in my own mind, I thought that I was dreaming again. Then I turned on the light and realized that this was the real thing. Don't ask me why, but the first thing I did was get up and shave. I had to make a couple of phone calls because not only did I have a ton of envelopes with tickets in them for doctors, nurses, and other people for games six and seven, but I also had received a phone call from a good friend of my brother's, and I was still looking for six tickets for game six for Joel Aranson.

I really hadn't had a chance to talk to my brother between the end of game five and this moment. After a game, a visiting team shows up, boards a flight and heads back. I called my friend Jerry Goldberg and gave him a long list of things to do, including calling my kids and everything. The hospital phone system was so complicated and Jerry had the only 800 number I could reach in the middle of the night. I gave him all the assignments to let everybody know what was happening.

Then about 6:30 a.m. in the morning, they came and got me. The first thing they do is shave you pretty much all over, clean you up, and then go over the details of what is going to take place. I had heard this on a number of occasions because they prepare you pretty well.

They informed me of the fact that when I first woke up after the operation that I'd be heavily sedated and that I would have a tube down my throat. I would be paralyzed. I would be blind. This was all normal, they're telling me.

Between people in white coats, male and female, including the surgeons moving around the room, they said they were going to put me under. I don't know how much time had gone by, probably a couple of hours by now, and I was downstairs in the operating room.

I didn't know and I'm not sure they knew specifically when they put me under that the donor was a 28-year old man from the Bronx who had a brain tumor. Not only was his wife agreeing to donate his heart to me, but a couple of his other organs were to go to other people as well. Therefore, the last thing they take out is the heart, since they have the shortest amount of time to work with it. As a result, I was under a little longer than they would have liked due to the fact that, whether it was a kidney or a liver or whatever the other two organs were, there were multiple donations from this man.

But I do know that three people's lives, including my own, were saved this particular night. I'm not exactly sure, because I was out cold when the operation began, but the next thing I knew, I was waking up just like they described in sort of a total daze, pretty well drugged up. I vaguely remember, and it was the presiding surgeon who said, "It's over. It took like a duck to water. Now go back to bed." Of course, I don't know if you call it going back to bed, because I was in bed, but I just passed back out again.

Oh, maybe it was four or five hours later before I woke up again, and now, even though I still couldn't see clearly, I could see little blocks of light and things and I could move the ends of my fingers and I had some movement. When I woke up, I could see the semblance of different people in the room and I heard my brother's voice.

He was standing there with Reggie Jackson, a dear friend of mine also, Matt Merola, who is Reggie's agent, and the two doctors. Don't ask me why, but I was trying to communicate with my brother about these tickets that this gentleman, Joel, needed for game six.

Eventually they brought me a piece of paper and a pencil, as though we were going to play charades, and I was trying to write it down, and my brother about half way through this exercise looks at it and said," Oh hell, he's alright, he's asking for tickets."

So apparently I communicated pretty well. The next time I woke up was in an intensive care unit, the tube had come out of my throat, and they told me that once the tube comes out of your throat, the heart is functioning on its own, which is a major step in the right direction. I really had no pain other than the fact that they had to crack the bone in my chest, but I was very stable.

As I found out later, there actually was more blood pulsing through my system now with the new heart than I had experienced in a long time. I was becoming alive again, but there was no time to gloat, because the next night brought game six. Joe and his Yankees could win it all.

I had pretty much come around, and I sat up slightly to watch, wired up to monitors pretty heavily. A couple of the doctors sat with me because I was considered a pretty important patient in terms of visibility.

Later that night, I learned that every network in the country had television cameras, vans, wagons, antennae, satellite dishes, whatever, waiting outside the hospital for whatever might transpire with Joe and me. I got clips and copies of all the coverage; I hadn't realized how much interest there had been.

I still haven't had the guts to go back and look at the actual surgery tape though. I can deal with almost anything, but I can't do that. No instant replay needed.

It was funny because that particular night, for inning after inning, they had me on the monitor, my blood pressure stayed steady, and my pulse was perfect. It didn't move the whole time.

Then comes the ninth inning. With my adrenaline pumping, the old blood pressure shot way up. Even the new heart had to respond to the emotion and the tension of the situation.

The doctor at my side said, "If you think this is bad, just imagine what it would have been like if we had your old heart in there now instead of the new one." I can only imagine. I think it would have burst.

So there I was, in complete comfort with a new heart, knowing everything that was going on, watching my brother and his New York Yankees win the World Series about 24 hours after I had conveniently received a new heart on an off day between Series games. It was like a fairy tale.

Extra Inning

FRANK TORRE'S MAJOR LEAGUE CAREER WAS *winding to a close just as his brother Joe's was taking off. They passed trajectories as Braves only briefly in 1960. Frank was forever proud of his big brotherly role in bringing Joe into the baseball fold.*

Throughout his baseball tenure, Frank had always possessed a keen instinct for business. Late in the 1957 championship season, he parlayed a pennant-clinching victory into a promotional opportunity for his client Pepsi Cola in the winner's clubhouse.

Once out of uniform and embarking on a new career as a businessman, he quickly hit his stride, and as an executive for Adirondack bats, began to challenge the venerable Louisville Slugger empire for supremacy of the major league bat market, exhibiting the same competitive spirit that defined his play.

Frank personally refined various processes to allow the hand-tailoring of bats for baseball stars in a touring "batmobile," using a special traveling lathe. He put stripes on Adirondack bats to distinguish them from competitor models. He lured some of the greatest hitters away from their traditional wood, and saw Willie Mays blast his 500th home run with an Adirondack in his hands.

In building business overseas, Frank directed visionary strategies that successfully opened up the Japanese market to American sporting goods, and baseball in particular.

In a business story that deserves case study status in business schools, Frank Torre directed Rawlings' effort to win the major league baseball "adoption" away from Spalding. For the entire history of baseball previously, Spalding had enjoyed the monopoly on manufacturing the baseball for major league play. Incredibly, when Frank arrived at Rawlings, he found Spalding to be quite complacent about this honor, and he set out to win the prize. Through sheer willpower, close friendships, precise study of the ball's specifications, acute understanding of what Major League Baseball wanted in its baseballs, and a bit of luck, Frank snared the right for Rawlings to make the balls used in the major leagues.

Following his heart transplant, Frank went on to watch his brother Joe manage the Yankees to three more championships—in 1998, 1999, and 2000, and then move west to manage the Los Angeles Dodgers from 2008 to 2010. Joe later became a top MLB executive, a position he still holds.

In 2007, Frank received a kidney transplant from one of his four daughters, Elizabeth, giving him seven more years of productive living to enjoy his children—Elizabeth, Margaret, Janet, Katherine, and Frank, Jr. Frank Jr. was named head baseball coach at Indian River State College in Florida in 2018, and with his wife Kelly, carries on the Torre baseball tradition coaching and through their two sons, Gavin and Rowen.

The great Milwaukee Braves first baseman Frank Torre stepped into the cornfields of time and joined the angels in the outfield at the age of 82 on September 13, 2014.

—Cornelius Geary

The Legend of Mel Fame

I T WAS BACK AT THE TURN OF THE century, 19-ought something it was, a little before or a little after, well into the gloaming, because they played without lights as night fell, when pitching great Mel Fame (pronounced Fay-mee) now largely lost to history last made his mark. Looking all that way back, they can barely tell us now if he was a lefty or a righty, even black or white. But it was a big game, everyone remembers. A very big game. A game that meant something. The winner went on.

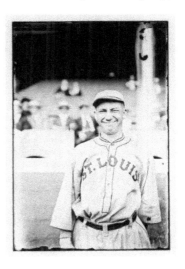

Now Mel had always been famous for the night before. And in his prime it never seemed to make no never mind. But later on it became an issue. Not at first. Sometimes Mel would walk right out onto the mound from the night before and shut them right down. Then later they had to roust him, point him out past the plate. Mostly beer it was. So this one night, with the score tied in the bottom of the 13th and the favorites being out on the road, and the moon already up, his manager had no choice but to bring him in, since all the other arms were beat, and Mel's was still live. It had been anything but a perfect game. It was either 10-10, or 8-8. Maybe even 12-12.

With nobody out and one man on, Mel walked the bases full. Then he got an out, and then another. It looked like Mel was seeing right through his haze from the night before and the curve was working nicely. But then off a full count he walked in the winning run. The curve just missed and the guy looked it in and took it. It was all over. The other team went on.

After the game, the guy from the *Trib*, or the *Sun*, or the *Sentinel*, asked the other manager, on the winning side—either Connie, or Casey or Mugsy, but maybe it was Biff—what had made the difference in the game? Without giving it a second thought, the winning manager replied as he unbuttoned his woolen jersey, with a gimlet eye to making sure the guy from the *Trib*, or the *Sun*, or the *Sentinel* was getting it down right,

"Without a doubt, it was the beer that made Mel Fame walk us."

Appendix

Photos courtesy of Richard Lulloff.

ENDNOTES

Most facts in this book were sourced from Baseball Reference (www.baseball-reference.com). For Frank Torre's major league record, type his name in the search box on that site. SABR Society for American Baseball Research, (SABR, www.sabr.org) also was an important reference.

[1] *New York Times*, Nov. 17, 1973.

[2] Office of the Mayor of New York City - Press Release, August 15, 1997.

[3] Society for American Baseball Research, Joe Adcock, par. 17.

[4] *New York Times*, April 17, 1972; Society for American Baseball Research, Lou Perini.

[5] *Milwaukee Journal Green Sheet* - Our Back Page, April 13, 2016.

[6] Baseball-Reference.com- Milwaukee Braves, year-by-year statistics, 1957

[7] *New York Times*, April 4, 1999.

[8] Baseball Prospectus - You Could Look It Up, John Quinn's Reign, by Steve Goldman, August 24, 2005.

[9] Society of American Baseball Research - Frank Torre - par. 14.

[10] *Hartford Courant,* Dom Amore - Oct. 19, 1996.

[11] *Fansided - Atlanta Braves History: Red Schoendienst and the 1957 World Series,* Fred Owens, 2018.

[12] *New York Times,* article by Ken Plutnicki - May 4, 2012.

[13] "The Deadball Era," Chuck Dressen, *New York Times,* August 11, 1966.

[14] "The Deadball Era," Birdie Tebbetts, March 26, 1999.

[15] *Milwaukee Journal Sentinel,* article by JR Radcliffe, April 6, 2018.

[16] Ballparksofbaseball.com, Atlanta Fulton County Stadium.

Index

Abbreviations "FT" and "JT" stand for Frank Torre and Joe Torre, respectively.

A

Aaron, Hank ("Hammerin' Hank")
    1957 season play, 68–72, 83, 89–91
    1957 World Series play, 95, 97, 99,
        101, 106–8, 114–15
    1958 season play, 117–20, 129, 139
    1958 World Series play, 141, 145,
        147, 150–52
    1959 early season play, 167–69
    1959 Playoff series, 170–72
    batting average, 54, 71
    breaking the home run record, 36
    comparison to Willie Mays, 131–36
    FT relationship/reflections, 4,
        42–44, 46
    Golden Glove award, 120
    home runs/MVP award, 68, *71*, *91*,
        107, 120, 132–36
    John A. "Bud" Hillerich Award, *173*
    JT relationship, 20
    photograph, *22*, *36*, *70*, *133*, *135*,
        137, *160*, *163*, *165*, *183*
Adams, Nick, 122–23
Adcock, Joe
    1957 season play, 75–77, 160
    1957 World Series play, 44, 95, 97,
        99, 106–7, 114
    1958, World Series play, 142, 147
    1959 season play, 165, 170
    batting average, 54
    change in playing position, 117,
        131, 168, 177
    FT playing backup to, 38–39, 46–49
    FT relationship/reflections, 59–62
    home runs, 48–49, 54, 60, *165*, 167
    injuries/broken leg, 38–39, 77, 85,
        88, 99, 102, 117
    photograph, *37*, *60*, *165*, *183*
Adirondack bats, 203
Alfonso, Edgardo, 78
All-Star player
    Birdie Tebbetts, *178*
    Bob Rush, *145*
    Bob Turley, *156*
    Bobby Thompson, *52*
    Don McMahon, *149*
    Ed Matthews, *72*
    Felix Mantilla, *104*
    Gene Conley, *121*
    Hank Bauer, *140*
    Harvey Haddix, 167
    Joe Adcock, *60*
    Joe Torre, 19
    Johnny Logan, *104*
    Mickey Mantle, *141*
    Orlando Cepeda, *119*
    Paul Waner, *159*
    "Pee Wee" Reese, *58*
    Phil Niekro, *180*
    Red Schoendienst, *125*
    Roger Maris, *143*
    Roy Campanella, *129*
    Sandy Koufax, *44*
    Stan Musial, 57
    Warren Spahn, 119
    Willie Mays, *130*
Antonelli, Johnny, 169
Ashburn, Richie, 76–77, *79*, 120
Atlanta Braves
    1966 move from Milwaukee, 40
    1996 World Series, 185–87, 198
Austin, Alan, 120
Avila, Bobby, 170

B

Baltimore Orioles, 72, 167, 177
Banks, Ernest ("Ernie"), 21, 42, 71, *78*,
    120, 169
baseball
    bunts, 47, 53, 89, 103, 105, 145, 153
    cars, gifts, free services, 61–68
    closing pitchers, 105, 198
    daylight games, 157
    ejections/bench-clearing fights, *55*,
        72–75
    ignoring/missing coaching signs,
        103, 110
    "pickle"/"stay in the pickle," 55–56,
        58
    player salary and World Series

bonus, 59, 115
sacrifice outs, 77, 89, 137, 167
scouts/scouting, 16, 19, 26, 59
Spring Training medical checkup,
  130–32
stealing bases, 133–34
stealing the signs, 75–77, 131
baseball, about the catcher position
  Bob Uecker as, 179–82
  Del Rice as, *157*
  JT potential as, 17
  requirements for, 18–19
  Roy Campanella as, *129*, 131
  stealing the signs, 75–77
  Yogi Berra, *43*, *159*
baseball, amateur, 17, 47
baseball, minor league, 5, 17, 24, 28, 31,
  35, 40, 46, 49, 79, 83, 164, 174,
  177–82
baseball, semi-pro, 11–12, 47
Baseball Hall of Fame
  Joe Torre, 19
  "Pee Wee" Reese, *58*
  Sandy Koufax, *44*
  Stan Musial, *43*
  Willie Mays, *130*
  Yogi Berra, *43*
Baseball Reference (website), 205
Bauer, Hank, 97, 101, 106–8, *140*,
  141–42, 147, 150
Berger, Cy, 187
Berra, Lawrence Peter ("Yogi"), 42, *43*,
  101–03, 142, 149–53, 155, *159*
Boston Braves, 12, 37, 41, 46–47, 104,
  164
Boston Celtics, 121, 122
Brooklyn Cadets, 17, *18*, 20
Brooklyn Dodgers, 42, 44, 52, 83, 98,
  129
Bruton, Bill, *42*, 46, 79, 83, 118–19,
  137, 141, 145, 147–49, 170, 172
Buhl, Bob, 54, *64*, 74–77, 98–99,
  107–8, 142, *162*, 172
Burdette, Selva Lewis ("Lew")
  1956 season play, 54
  1957 season play, 68, 83
  1957 World Series play, 96–97,
    106–10, 114–15
  1958, season play, 117
  1958, World Series play, 141–42,
    145, 155
  1958 World Series play, 148–52
  1959, Playoff series, 169, 172

Beverly Hills pool party, 121–23
FT relationship/reflections, 36, 42
photograph, *64*, *109*, *113*, *160*
as team joker/clown, 69–50, 137–40
Byrne, Tommy, 99

C

Campanella, Roy ("Campy"), *55*, *56*,
  129, 131
Cepeda, Orlando, 5, 42, *119*, 120, 169
Chandler, Jeff, 124–25
Chapman, Lou, *65*, *66*, 169
Chicago Cubs, 46, 49, 76–78, 82, 83,
  120, 169
Churn, Clarence ("Chuck"), 172
Cincinnati Reds, 46, 71–74, 82, 167
Clemente, Roberto, *40*, 42, 70, 132
Cleveland Indians, 12, 130, 178
Cobb, Ty, *68*
Columbia Presbyterian Hospital,
  187–202
Conley, Gene, *64*, 98–99, *121*,
  121–23, *136*
Cottier, Chuck, *163*
Covington, John Wesley ("Wes"), 42, 46,
  63, 79, 83, *91*, 95–97, 106–07, 114,
  138, 145, 147, 150–53, 160, 169–70,
  176
Crandall, Del, 36, 44–45, *64*, 109, *113*,
  141, 145, 151, 160, 170, 172, *183*
Crowe, George, 46, *47*, 50, 71, 81, 83
Cy Young Award, 44, 68

D

Davidson, Donald, 137–38
Del Greco, Bobby, 51–53
Denver Bears, 5, 20, 24, 35
Detroit Tigers, 72, 82, 83–84, 178
Dickson, Murry, 146–47
Ditmar, Art, 97
Dittmer, Jack, 49–51
Donatelli, Augie, 102–03
Drabowsky, Myron W. ("Moe"), 180, *182*
Dressen, Charlie ("Chuck"), *174*,
  175–78
Drysdale, Don, 43, 71, 169–72
Duren, Ryne, 142, 147, 150

E

Ebbets Field, 17, 48, 56, 131
Evans, Craig, 187

F

Ferguson, Tommy, 21–*22*, 103, *160*
fights/ejections, *55*, 72–74
Fonda, Jane, 186
Ford, Whitey, 4, 42–43, 93, 95–96,
   106–07, 114, 141, 147, 154
Forester, Bill, 127
free cars, gifts and services, 61–68
Friend, Bob, 43

G

Gehrig, Henry Louis ("Lou"), 173
Gillespie, Earl, *183*
The Godfather (movie series), 4, 28
Goldberg, Jerry, 199
Golden Glove award, hits and misses
   Ed Matthews, 71
   Gil Hodges, 39
   Hank Aaron, 120, 169
   Harvey Haddix, 167
Green Bay Packers, 126–28, *183*
Grim, Bob, 97, 99, 103, 106
Grimm, Charlie, *41*, 46, 49–50, 59

H

Haddix, Harvey, 44, 60, *165–65*, 167
Hanebrink, Harry, 148, *164*
Haney, Fred, *22*, 49–*50*, 59, *68*, *93*, 99,
   103–05, 110, 117–18, 124, 146,
   150–51, 170
Hazle, Bob ("Hurricane"), 79, 81–85,
   114–15, 160
Hernandez, Keith, 136
Hill, Dan, 17
Hillerich, John A. ("Bud"), 173
Hodges, Gilbert R. ("Gil"), 4, *39*, 42, 71,
   106, *135*, 136, 170–72
Hornung, Paul, 125–28, 178–79
Houk, Ralph, 144
Houston Astros, 72
Howard, Elston, 101, 106, 149–50, 156

J

Jackson, Reggie, 200
Japan, baseball in, 5, 203
Jay, Joseph R. ("Joey"), 76–77, *81*
John A. "Bud" Hillerich Award, *173*
Johnson, Ernie, 95, 99, 108, *164*
Jolly, Dave, *174*
Jones, Vernal ("Nippy"), 44, *85*, 88, *102*,
   115, *160*

K

Kansas City Athletics, 12
Knippel-Sigel Ford (car dealership),
   64–66
Korean War, 6, 35
Koufax, Sandy, 43, *44*, 169, 172
Kubek, Tony, 96, 98, 99, 101, 109, *110*
Kucks, Johnny, 99, 146–47

L

Labine, Clement ("Clem"), 172
Larker, Norm, 170
Larsen, Don, 42–43, *98*, 99, 108,
   114–15, 146–48, 151
Lewis, Duffy, *68*
Logan, Johnny, 42, 78–79, 83, 92,
   95–97, 99, 103–06, *104*, 114–15, 121,
   145, 147, *161*, 170–72
Lombardi, Vincent ("Vince"), 126–28
Los Angeles Dodgers, 44, 56–58, 120,
   124, 169–72, 175–76, 204
Louisville Colonels, 40, 177–82
Louisville Slugger (bats), 203

M

Maas, Duke, 142, 146
MacLean, Raymond T. ("Scooter"), 126
Mafia (mob), presence/influence in
   baseball, 27–28
Maglie, Salvatore ("Sal"), 43
Mantilla, Felix, 60, *91*, 103, *104*, 119,
   128, 160, *163*, 165, 167, 171
Mantle, Mickey, 4, 42, 99, *141*,
   142–46, 173
Maris, Roger, *143*, 144, 173
Martin, Billy, 144–45
Mathews, Edwin ("Eddie")
   1957 season play, 68, 78, 83
   1957 World Series play, 104–06,
      111
   1958, World Series play, 145, 156
   1958 season play, 117–18
   1958 World Series play, 147
   1959, Playoff series, 169
   baseball skills/competitive nature,
      71–75
   batting order, 89
   FT relationship/reflections, 4, 36, 42
   Mel Ott Award, *173*
   photograph, *37*, *73*, *183*

Mays, Willie
  1957 MVP race, 71
  1958 season play, 120
  1959 season play, 169
  comparison to Hank Aaron, 131–36
  comparison to Mantle, 144
  FT relationship/reflections, 4, 42
  home run record, 175, 203
  JT relationship, 21
  photograph, *130*, *160*
McBride, George, *68*
McCovey, Willie, 5, 173
McDevitt, Danny, 170
McDougald, Gilbert ("Gil"), 101, 106,
  142, 148–50, *151*
McElroy, Jim, 17
McMahon, Don, 42, *64*, 76, 96, 98,
  146–47, *149*, *162*, 172, *174*
Mel Ott Award, *173*
Merola, Matt, 200
Miami Marlins, 12
Milwaukee Braves
  1953-55, arrival in Milwaukee, 36,
    41–42
  1956-60, the "glory years," 35–45
  1956 and the "September Swoon,"
    45–48
  1957, play during the season, 59–90
  1957, winning the pennant, 90–92
  1957, winning the World Series
    Game 1, 93–96
    Game 2, 96–97
    Game 3, 98–99
    Game 4, 99–06
    Game 5, 106–07
    Game 6, 107–08
    Game 7, 108–15, 186–87
  1958, play during the season,
    117–40
  1958, World Series
    Game 1, 141–42
    Game 2, 142–46
    Game 3, 146–47
    Game 4, 147
    Game 5, 148–49
    Game 6, 149–50
    Game 7, 150–57
  1959, play during the season,
    167–69
  1959, Playoff series
    Game 1, 169–70
    Game 2, 170–72
  1960, end of the championship era,
    175–77

1966, move to Atlanta, 40
attendance figures, 40–41, 53, 93,
  97
Milwaukee Brewers (Minor League), 41
Milwaukee County Stadium, 36, 75,
  101, 167, *183*
Monroe, Zachary ("Zach"), 146
Moon, Wally, 92, 170
Most Valuable Player (MVP), hits and
misses
  Bob Turley, *156*
  Ed Matthews, 71, 72
  Ernie Banks, 71, 120, 169
  Frank Robinson, 72
  Gil Hodges, 71
  Hank Aaron, 68, *71*
  Joe Torre, 7, 19
  Lew Burdette, 113
  Mickey Mantle, *141*
  Paul Waner, *159*
  Red Schoendienst, 71
  Roberto Clemente, 40
  Roger Maris, *143*
  Roy Campanella, 55
  Sandy Koufax, *44*
  Stan Musial, *57*, 71
  Warren Spahn, 71
  Willie Mays, 73, *130*
Muffett, Billy, 91
Musial, Stan, 21, 42, *43*, 54–57, 71, 120

N

National League pennant
  1951 NY Giants v. Brooklyn
    Dodgers, 52, 53, 76, 83, 174
  1952 NY Giants v. Brooklyn
    Dodgers, 174
  1953 Milwaukee Braves v. Brooklyn
    Dodgers, 174
  1956 Milwaukee Braves "September
    Swoon," 35, 49–58
  1957 Milwaukee Braves v. St. Louis
    Cardinals, 39, 90–92
  1959 Milwaukee Braves v. Los
    Angeles Dodgers, 36, 40
Neal, Charlie, 170
New York Giants, 42, 52–53, 70, 83, 174
New York Mets, 78
New York Yankees
  1956 World Series, 39, 98
  1957 World Series, 3, 5, 35, 44, 50,
    84, 93–115, 164
  1958 World Series, 35, 39–40, 44,
    98, 141–57

1960 World Series, 167
1996 World Series, 5, 185–87,
192–93, 198–202
Joe Torre as manager, 19, 45, 185,
193
Newcomb, Don, 43
Niekro, Phil, 181, *181*

O

O'Connell, Danny, *54*
Ott, Mel, 80, 173

P

Pafko, Andy, *64*, 95, 107, 114, 147, *175*
Paige, Leroy ("Satchel"), *12*
Palmer, Arnold, 192
Pepsi Cola, FT post-transplant career,
203–04
Perini, Charles, *41*
Perini, Lou, *41*
Petitte, Andy, 198
Philadelphia Phillies, 62, 70, 79, 84,
167, 182
Pittsburgh Pirates, 40, 44, 60, 159, 165,
167
Pizzaro, Juan, 98, 148
Podres, Johnny, 43, 69–70, 131, 168,
172

Q

Quinn, John, 59, *62*

R

Rank, Wally, *64*
Rawlings Sporting Goods Company, 5,
203–04
Reese, Harold Henry ("Pee Wee"/the
Colonel), 57–58
Rice, Del, *157*
Richardson, Bobby, *151*
Roberts, Robin, 43
Robinson, Frank, 42, 71–74, 132
Robinson, Humberto, *80*
Robinson, Jack Roosevelt ("Jackie"), 42,
54–55, *56*, 58
Roseboro, John, 170
Rush, Bob, *133*, *145*, 146–47, 172
Russell, John ("Honey"), 19
Ruth, George Herman ("Babe"), 36, 143,
159, 173

S

San Francisco Giants, 72, 120, 128, 130,
131, 169, 174
Schabowski, Rick, 6
Schoendienst, Albert Fred ("Red")
1957 season play, 70–71, 83, 88–89,
160
1957 World Series play, 99, 115
1958 season play, 117–98
1958 World Series play, 145, 147
Beverly Hills pool party, 121–23
diagnosed with tuberculosis, 128–30
FT relationship/reflections, 42
photograph, *64*, *125*, *133*
Sears, Roebuck & Co., 5
Selig, Ben, 64–66
Selig, Bud ("Buddy"), 64–67, 91, 101,
177
Shantz, Bobby, 97, 99, *100*, 109
Sherry, Larry, 170
"Shot Heard 'Round the World," 52
Skowron, Bill ("Moose"), *111*, 141–42,
149, 151–52
Slaughter, Enos, 97, 107
Snider, Duke, 20, 42
Society for American Baseball Research
(SABR), 205
The Sopranos (TV series), 4
Spahn, Warren ("Spahnnie")
1956 season play, 54
1957 season play, 71, 83
1957 World Series play, 93, 95,
104–06, 108, 124–25
1958 season play, 117, 119–20
1958 World Series play, 141–42,
147–51
1959 season play, 169, 172
1960 season play, 175–76
Cy Young Award, 68
FT relationship/reflections, 4, 36,
42, 55, 57
photograph, *37*, *64*, *92*, *148*, *161*,
161
as team joker/clown, 69–50, 137–40
Spalding (sporting goods company),
203, 204
Sports Illustrated, 37
St. Louis Browns, 156
St. Louis Cardinals, 12, 46, 51, 54–55,
82, 84, 90–92, 167, 176, 186

Steinbrenner, George, 185
Stengel, Charles ("Casey"), *93*, 97, 112
Stone, Harvey, 179
Sturdivant, Tom, 99–101, 106, 114

T

Tanner, Chuck, *54*
Tebbetts, George ("Birdie"), 71, 177–79
Thompson, Bobby, *52*–53, 75
Tobe, Warner, 121–23
Toledo Mud Hens, 5, 35, 45
Torre, Frank
    about the interview for this book, 3–7
    Army service in Korea, 6, 35
    death, 204
    declining health, 187–91
    preparation for transplant, 191–97
    transplant operation, 197–202
    work career after the transplant, 3–5, 203–04
Torre, Frank, MLB career
    1956-60, Milwaukee "glory" year reflections, 35–45
    1956 Milwaukee rookie year, 35, 45–58
    1957 World Series win, 59–92
    as part of Braves history, 7
    batting average, 53–54, 177
    home runs, 38, 44, 99–100, 107–8, 118
    minor league, coming up, 5–6, 35, 40, 45
    minor league, sent back down, 174, 177–82
    photograph, *80*, *85–87*, *113*, *116*
    player salary and World Series bonus, 59, 115
    playing for the Phillies, 42, *182*
    playing with injuries, 85, 87
    post-transplant career, 204
Torre, Joe (father, "King Joe"), 9–16, 22–34, 108
Torre, Joseph Paul ("Joe")
    about the interview for this book, 3
    family and father relationship, 15–30, 30–33
    FT relationship/mentoring, 5–7, 17–21, 24–30, 45, 156–57, 177, 187–89, 193–95, 203
    managing the Yankees, 19, 45, 185, 193
    photograph, *31*, *161*

    playing for Milwaukee, 19, *116*, *179*
    visiting hospitalized children, 195
    Yankees '96 World Series, 5, 185–87, 193, 198, 201–02
Torre, Marge, 31–34
Torre, Marguerite, 11, 22–24, 29–30, 94
Torre, Rae, 3, 11, *23*–24, 27–31, 187, 194
Torre, Rocco, 11–12, 16, 26–27, 29–33
Trowbridge, Bob, 98, 99
Turley, Bob, 43, 98–99, 107–08, 114, 142, 146, 148–49, 151, 155, *156*
Turner, Ted, 186

U

Uecker, Bob, 43, 49, 70, 179–82, 190

W

Waner, Paul, 5–6, *159*
Wichita Braves, 5, 81–82, 83
Wilhelm, Hoyt, 43
Willey, Carlton, 146, 148, *150*, 170
Williams, Stan, 172
Williams, Ted, 5
Winters, Lee, 120
World Series
    1948 Cleveland Indians v. Boston Braves, 12
    1954 NY Giants v. Cleveland Indians, 130
    1956 NY Yankees v. Brooklyn Dodgers, 39, 98
    1957 Milwaukee Braves v. NY Yankees, 3, 5, 35, 44, 50, 84, 93–115, 164
    1958 NY Yankees v. Milwaukee Braves, 35, 39–40, 44, 98, 139–57
    1960 Pittsburgh Pirates v. NY Yankees, 167
    1996 NY Yankees v. Atlanta Braves, 5, 185–86, 192–93, 198–202
    Brooklyn Dodgers, 58
    Chicago Cubs, 49
    Los Angeles Dodgers, 44
    players' bonus, 115

Z

Zeidler, Frank, *41*

About the Author

CORNELIUS GEARY WAS BORN IN MILWAUKEE, Wisconsin, raised in Wauwatosa, and attended Marquette University High School. He received a BA (*cum laude*) from the University of Wisconsin–Milwaukee and an MA from the University of Southern California. He was Midwest Editor for *National Petroleum News*, Director of Marketing Communications for Amoco Corporation, and General Manager of Government and Public Affairs for BP.

He is the author of *Bastion*, the streaming series, *Cheeseheads, The Ogallala, The Shrine, Peekaboo,* and *Over Easy*, all screenplays, and the stage play, *A Pot to Piss In, The Fall of Europe, Ireland on the Brink*. He resides with his wife Sandra in Galveston, Texas. His children Elizabeth and John live in Chicago, and his son Con resides in San Francisco. He remains loyal to the Packers, Brewers, and Bucks.

Contact information:
Email: gearlit@gmail.com
Facebook: CorneliusGearyAuthor

CPSIA information can be obtained
at www.ICGtesting.com
Printed in the USA
FFHW010122130619
52968439-58580FF